"The combination of inspiration, motiv... perfect blend for first-time entrepreneurs."

—*Success* magazine

"*Your Idea, Inc.* is a lively, informative weekend workshop rolled into a paperback. Sandy Abrams has written an indispensable step-by-step guide for anyone even casually considering developing their business idea into a reality. Her mix of practical advice and information with inspiring start-up stories demystifies the process of birthing a new business and makes the prospect far less daunting. Abrams is savvy and experienced, and a highly effective cheerleader for all of us who dream of independence and financial success."

—Meg Cadoux Hirshberg, Columnist for *Inc.* magazine

"Passion trumps experience. *Your Idea, Inc.* gives first time entrepreneurs the immediate advice needed to get started and follow their dreams."

—Michael Greenberg, President, Skechers, USA

"No need to keep that great idea locked up in your head any longer! *Your Idea, Inc.* inspires first-time entrepreneurs to just roll up their sleeves and get started no matter how limited the resources or experience."

—Jane Buckingham, Founder, "The Intelligence Group" Trendforecasting Company

"Inspirational! Sandy shares her entrepreneurial secrets in this authentic and motivational book. Makes you feel like you can achieve your own business aspirations. A "must-read" for the Modern Mom."

—Lisa Rosenblatt, Co-CEO ModernMom.com

"Sandy Abrams offers a step-by-step guide for starting your own business that lays bare many of the challenges new entrepreneurs face and then gives advice on how to overcome them. This 12-step program is a clear and concise resource for aspiring business owners."

—Jess Weiner, Self-Esteem Expert and Author of *A Very Hungry Girl* and *Life Doesn't Begin 5 Pounds from Now*

"After reading this book, I wish I'd had this book when I started in business. A great resource!!!"

—Jackie Applebaum, CEO Privé Products

your

**12 Steps
to Building a
MILLION-DOLLAR
Business—Starting
Today!**

idea, inc.

Sandy Abrams,
founder and CEO of Moisture Jamzz, Inc.

Aadamsmedia
Avon, Massachusetts

Published by
Adams Media, a division of F+W Media, Inc.
57 Littlefield Street, Avon, MA 02322. U.S.A.
www.adamsmedia.com

ISBN 10: 1-59869-909-1
ISBN 13: 978-1-59869-909-8

Printed in the United States of America.

J I H G F E D C B A

Library of Congress Cataloging-in-Publication Data
is available from the publisher.

This publication is designed to provide accurate and authoritative information
with regard to the subject matter covered. It is sold with the understanding that
the publisher is not engaged in rendering legal, accounting, or other professional
advice. If legal advice or other expert assistance is required, the services of a competent professional person should be sought.
—From a *Declaration of Principles* jointly adopted by a Committee of the
American Bar Association and a Committee of Publishers and Associations

Many of the designations used by manufacturers and sellers to distinguish their
product are claimed as trademarks. Where those designations appear in this book
and Adams Media was aware of a trademark claim, the designations have been
printed with initial capital letters.

This book is available at quantity discounts for bulk purchases.
For information, please call 1-800-289-0963.

*This book is dedicated to all the "underdogs" in business,
people who dared to beat the odds and follow their dream.*

contents

acknowledgments

Thank you, Meredith Jacobs, for leading me in the right direction and introducing me to Joanne Brownstein. You have been the best mentor. But more than that, your true friendship, generosity, honesty, humor, and enthusiasm have meant so much to me.

Thank you, Joanne Brownstein of Brandt and Hochman Literary Agents. You just "got it." You heard my passion and you took the time to bring it into focus. You worked above and beyond the call of duty with my proposal, to shape this book into what it is. Most importantly, you found a publisher. I am eternally grateful.

Thank you, Andrea Norville, my wonderful editor, for believing in this book's potential and dealing with this first-time author who is not a writer. Your patience and kindness will not be forgotten.

A very grateful thank you to Wendy Simard, Laura Daly, and Laurel Marotta for organizing my thoughts and giving this book clarity. Thank you to Paula Munier at Adams Media as well; all of the support has been tremendous!

Thank you, Darryn Eller, for your positive reinforcement years ago. Those kind words coming from such a pro meant a lot to me and gave me the confidence to believe I could see this in the bookstores one day.

Thank you to all the entrepreneurs who inspired me along the way. I am always attracted to the underdog stories, the unlikely candidates who become big successes. Those people were powerful examples and really gave me strength to believe that I could do it too.

To Brock and Clay, I hope you follow your dreams and eventually earn a living doing something that you are passionate about. All my love to you!

The biggest thank you goes to my husband, Ron Abrams. Your calm and wise nature has always helped to balance my enthusiasm and energy, and actually turn them into tangible results. I benefit daily from your love, humor, generosity, and your sage advice. I will never forget the day in 1995 when you turned in your resignation to the law firm, and we took the leap of faith that this "business thing" will be just fine. It's been so much fun having you by my side at Moisture Jamzz. You have been the best partner ever, and the kids and I are so happy and blessed with you around all the time! Thank you for believing. You know how much I love you!

Without the success of Moisture Jamzz, Inc., I would not have had a platform for this book. To Maria and Saul Vaquero, you have been with us since the very beginning, and I cannot thank you enough for always being there and for providing quality and conscientious work. You are two of the sweetest people Ron and I have ever met. We will always be grateful for your loyalty.

Thank you, Mom, for managing our office for ten years and for letting us vacation without worry. You were there every day with a smile, and you also offered us continuous support and love. Being able to count on you meant so much to us. You are such a blessing not only for Ron and me, but of course, for your grandkids too! We all love you so much and will always treasure that quality time that we had with you.

Mia Ruiz, we cannot thank you enough for your love and generosity. You became part of our family and you will always be a big part of our lives. You mean the world to all of us, and we could not have done as well without you. We love you and all of your family very much.

A huge and very grateful thank-you as well to West, Deborah, Jeffrey, Kenneth, Terree, and all of our production team. It is a true pleasure to work with you. Your support and dedication has enabled us to grow and thrive. Last, but surely not least, thank you from the bottom of my heart to each and every one of our customers.

seize your light bulb moment

In 1993, my life changed. A light bulb went off in my head as I had an incredible idea for a beauty product.

It all began because I had really dry, chapped hands and my grandmother suggested I put Vaseline on them and then wear white cotton gloves overnight. It was a beauty secret very familiar to the older generation. I searched beauty-conscious Los Angeles and could only find one type of moisturizing glove. It was a cheap, thin all-cotton glove that fell off within seconds of putting it on my hand. Again and again, I tried to follow my grandmother's advice, but I needed a better glove and I couldn't find one anywhere. That's when it hit me. I couldn't be the *only* one with dry hands looking for an easy remedy. As a result, I launched Moisture Jamzz, Inc., a bath and body manufacturer and wholesaler built around my signature product, Moisture Jamzz Moisture Gloves.

So how did I go from having that idea to being the founder of my own company? My journey was complicated at times, but it started with basic elements: excitement, ambition, and enthusiasm. When the light bulb went off, I knew I had to act on my idea. Like you, I dreamed of turning my simple concept into a business. I had the motivation, but I didn't have a clue about how to start a business. What I did have in my corner was my eternal optimism and naiveté. I just figured I could do it.

I did need somewhere to start, though. So I hit the bookstores for guidance and picked out several business start-up books with catchy titles. Unfortunately, I didn't find the help I needed in those books. I found the pages of dry information difficult to read, and I quickly became bogged down in all the financial and legal intricacies of business ownership. It's not that those things aren't important; they are, but nothing kills enthusiasm faster than complicated business jargon, most of which was completely foreign to me at the time. In the beginning, I didn't need to understand formal corporate structure because I was the entire organization.

So I returned to the bookstore in search of a comprehensive guide I could understand without having an MBA that would teach me the basics. I also needed help planning my work, staying motivated, and keeping track of what I'd done. No book I saw filled all those needs. Much like the light bulb moment that inspired me to create Moisture Jamzz, I figured that if the book I needed didn't exist, I'd have to create one.

Along with making notes in this book, I recommend that you also get a journal or binder or create a file on your computer specifically for notes and inspiration pertaining to your idea. In each chapter, you'll find exercises to help you get creative and organize your thoughts. When you see the words "Biz Brainstorm," it's time to get busy on your exercises! Every Biz Brainstorm is designed to get you thinking about your business, challenge your boundaries, and motivate you to take action.

The only difference between you and a successful entrepreneur is *action*. This book is rooted in that principle and will help you move from thought to action as painlessly as possible. So before you realize it, you'll be well on your way to launching your product. Whether you are a teacher, a chef, a stay-at-home mom, or a truck driver, a great idea is a great idea. You are qualified in your own way to join the ranks of every other entrepreneur who started out with only a dream.

Some people might tell you it is impossible to start a business from scratch without a business degree. Little do they know that some of the biggest names in business did not even have college degrees when they started their companies! What they did have is passion, just like you.

Check out some business owners who don't have business degrees:

- Mary Kay Ash, Mary Kay cosmetics
- Michael Dell, Dell Computers
- Debbie Fields, Mrs. Fields Cookies
- Bill Gates, Microsoft
- Milton Hershey, Hershey Chocolate
- Steve Jobs, Apple Computers

Even though I felt deeply unqualified at times, I never listened to the naysayers, and neither should you. I followed my instincts. I never felt there was anything strange about being the shipping clerk, accountant, sales manager, receptionist, account rep, and marketing person all rolled into one. I had no choice; I simply did it. I woke up each morning excited to continue my journey; I went to bed reviewing my workbook progress and dreaming about what could happen the next day.

Like me, if you don't have any business experience but you have a great product idea, congratulations! You have found the book that will get you started—no business degree required. This is the "learn as you go" plan. I am certainly not the most successful, most well-known, nor the most intelligent entrepreneur that ever lived. But I do bring my no-nonsense approach to this book, and that is something you won't find in many other business books. My approach will help get you started immediately so you can make tangible progress even as you read through these pages.

It's okay if you don't have an MBA. It's okay if you don't have a college degree. If you are seeking permission to enter the business world, you have it. It is not a club that requires education, status, or experience. This is a club you can join simply by following your dream and making it happen. The choice is yours. Choose action.

STEP 1

take the leap to becoming an entrepreneur

The secret of getting ahead is getting started. The secret of getting started is breaking down your complex overwhelming tasks into small manageable tasks, and then starting on the first one.

—MARK TWAIN

On the journey to launch a product idea, the very first step is often the most difficult to take. Why is that? Because you have to know what the first step *is*. Most people who have never run a business have absolutely no clue what to do with their great idea. Instead of focusing on only step number one, they start to paint a big picture, get overwhelmed mentally, and tuck the idea back into their head.

Sound familiar?

It's Time to Take Action, Even in a Bad Economy!

Ups and downs in the economy can seem scary, but it's possible to still earn a living and break out on your own. Even if the economy is unpredictable, you may find that these unexpected circumstances may very well lead to unexpected success and happiness.

It's not easy to see the glass half full right after being laid off, but once the dust has settled, you can join those entrepreneurs whose businesses thrived despite the tough economic times in which they were started. If you find yourself suddenly without work, dig deep inside yourself and try to embrace the opportunity to take charge of your own destiny. When life hands you lemons, make lemonade!

In a down economy, you might turn to entrepreneurship for one of the following reasons:

- You don't want to be at the mercy of a big corporation.
- You view a layoff as an overdue second chance in life to follow a dream you have let slip by.
- You want to go back to basics and simplicity. You are choosing "passion over paycheck" by changing professions completely. Starting a business may not be financially rewarding quickly, but in the long run, to feel passionate about your work for possibly the first time in your life is priceless. It's inspiring to see people choose an entirely new career, like going from being a stressed-out stock broker to a flour-covered pastry chef.
- You may need to bring in a second income because of the uncertainty of your spouse's work situation, so you are opting to do something on your own terms.
- You don't want to compete with other applicants for limited job opportunities.
- As an employee for most of your life, you want to utilize your vast experience and talents by becoming your own boss.

Starting a company during a downturn or even during the Depression has been done before with very successful results. In fact, sixteen of the thirty companies that make up the Dow Jones Industrial Average started under those difficult circumstances. These big names include Johnson & Johnson, Procter & Gamble, McDonald's, and Disney. This may be enough proof that there is not a bad time to start a good company!

You can't always pick the "right" time to become an entrepreneur. Usually new product ideas come about from a need to fill a void in the marketplace. For the entrepreneur, if the sense of urgency exists, the process begins organically no matter the state of the economy. It takes time to do the research and line up the ducks in a row from patents and trademarks to manufacturing and marketing. Who knows, by the time you are ready to launch, the economy and marketplace might have improved and you'll be in a great position to succeed.

Also, being in recession mode can actually help you adopt a "less is more" philosophy at the start of your business that continues when times get better. That is, you will naturally start small and expand when the time is right instead of biting off more than you can chew at the outset. This will be a great overall benefit to the financial health of your company.

If they can do it, So Can you!

The San Francisco–based Method Company's cleaning products can be found in just about every mass-market retailer today. But this $100 million-dollar company began just as the Internet's "dot-com bubble" had burst and the Bay Area was in a serious recession. The founders, Eric Ryan and Adam Lowry, who began by mixing batches of cleaning formula in their bathtub, found themselves drowning in debt. Having maxed out their credit cards and months overdue on paying their vendors, they kept pounding the pavement. With constant focus on their goal, within a year they were selling their Method products in 800 stores, including Target. Despite the recession, these two entrepreneurs have "cleaned up."

Be Positive and Proactive

In this economy, misery loves company. You can get caught up in the negativity and let opportunities pass because you are letting outside circumstances dictate your destiny. But that's not my way of living and because you are reading this book, it's probably not yours either. No matter what the economy is like, focus on what you *can* do and take action, and progress will build from momentum, optimism, and enthusiasm. Being positive and proactive, taking charge of your life is very empowering. When you love your work, it's no longer work! It's no secret that having a purpose in life makes you happier and more productive.

Good Reasons to Launch Your Idea in a Bad Economy

- Companies in manufacturing are hurting. They need to find new business now so they are likely to be more flexible with minimums. They will welcome a small business whereas in a thriving economy they will talk only to companies that will be spending a lot of money each and every month. You can start to build a relationship and grow your business as the economy improves.
- Companies across the board are offering better pricing to bring in business. You can take advantage of lower-than-usual pricing on everything from raw materials to office supplies.
- Talented people who were laid off from huge companies are now starting to consult on their own and charging a reasonable rate for their expertise. Take advantage of this trend by talking with an attorney, accountant, or graphic designer now working under his own shingle who can charge a much more reasonable hourly rate.
- The competition has been shrinking, so by the time you are in the marketplace, your company will be fresh and new and ready to do business from a solid foundation.
- Having fewer resources will force an entrepreneur to do more analytical thinking about streamlining expenses from the get-go. Instead of hiring people to work for you, outsource. Hiring independent contractors frees you up from having to worry

about offering expensive benefits such as health insurance. The tighter you can "run your ship" from the beginning stages, the better your profit margins will be in the long run.

Besides a bad economy, there's an endless list of reasons or excuses why most people don't follow through with their great ideas. For some, it's a matter of laziness or a lack of desire to complete a task or project. For others, a deeper fear of failing prevents them from ever taking action. Others just feel downright unqualified or even foolish to think they can launch a product with no experience.

To these people I say abandon that thought right now and listen to me. I had no business experience either, but I did it! Most people are capable of running a business if they have the passion to do so. It's like sports. You dedicate yourself to learn, train, and become the best you can be. Everyone has strengths and weaknesses. Take an objective look at yourself and identify yours. What kind of person are you? If you start something, will you finish it? When you get frustrated, can you find a way to forge ahead without giving up? Do you have enough discipline to make your own plan and follow it? If you believe that you can do this, you can do it. It's that simple.

If you've had your idea for a while and not acted on it until now, consider why. What obstacles stood in your way? Were they mental blocks? Or did they stem from a lack of confidence? If you can identify them, you can overcome them. If you allow it, you will always find excuses that prevent you from taking the first step, so strike them from your mental vocabulary. Instead, look for solutions. Be active, be aggressive, and be positive.

My hunch is that many more successful products have been developed by creative people than by businesspeople. We are all consumers. We know what we like to buy and what makes us pull out our wallet. If we like a product, we are not concerned with who created it; we just want it. If your idea will help your own life in some way and you'd be willing to pay for the product, chances are others will purchase it too.

The point is this: We are all uniquely qualified to be entrepreneurs. It's not courtroom litigation, where procedure is critical. A sure-fire plan, formula, or recipe is always nice, but the process of launching a product is different for everyone. The way you launch yours will be yet another unique road taken to the marketplace, and I hope to give you a map to help get you there.

Use Your Idea to Live the American Dream

Let's face it: We all want to earn a living doing something that we enjoy. I think most people would rather be their own boss—selling a product they created and love—than make millions doing someone else's bidding. For many people, that personal freedom is the "American Dream."

It's happening all over the country right now and not just by people who were laid off but by those driven by passion to give their dream a shot. People are running businesses from their homes, making calls from the bedroom closet, shipping inventory from the garage, and mixing batches of candle wax or lotion in the kitchen. According to the Small Business Administration, home-based businesses make up 53 percent of all small business.

So, as you clear that spot in your bedroom or your family room to set up your new venture, do it with pride. You are taking action and following your dreams. You are in your own office. You are your own boss. You are an entrepreneur.

Take a Leap of Faith

After years of working hard and watching higher-ups and big companies benefit most, many people are saying, "Enough is enough. I want to work hard for myself now."

I know people who are dissatisfied with their jobs but feel trapped. Quitting could bring freedom, independence, and ultimately happiness, but the fear of what might go wrong is strong enough to keep them in their jobs.

I also meet many stay-at-home moms who want to continue to be there for their kids, but are bored and a bit unfulfilled after their youngest is in kindergarten. These moms are looking for a part-time job so they can make some money and better utilize their newfound free time. These opportunities are often tough to uncover, but if you have a good product idea, you can be your own boss, work out of your home, be there for your family, and earn some money, too.

The American Dream is still possible to attain today, especially when you consider how technology makes it easy to start a business and have a virtual office that is professional and quick and inexpensive to set up.

Banish the Doubts

Merely *thinking* about the ways your life could improve, as you will in the Biz Brainstorm: What Does Success Mean to You? (next page) won't make them happen, of course. You may need to convince the practical side of your brain that is worried about bills, stability, and the future. To overcome those doubts, allow yourself to believe that you really do need a change and that you are capable of implementing it, one step at a time. Jess Weiner, author and motivational speaker, says, "Your body knows you have a great idea before your brain knows." This is so true. I know firsthand about the "fire in the belly" feeling. It's this adrenaline that keeps you taking step after step to make it happen, regardless of what your brain is saying in the background.

In order to silence the doubts the practical side of your brain may have, you'll need to maintain a healthy outlook. Let's look at how to do that.

Try Visualization

A helpful way to think positively is to visualize your success. Envision yourself as the person you hope to be—actually wearing that special suit and meeting that big client. Envision yourself in front of

What Does Success Mean to You?

Everyone's definition of success is different. Is it a dollar amount? Is it a lifestyle change? Being able to provide for loved ones? Feeling independent? What do you feel like you have to accomplish before you consider yourself "successful"? To harness these answers, make a two-column list. In the left column, write down everything you dislike about your current situation and the way it makes you feel. Think about every aspect of your current work life or your last job, such as:

- How you feel when you wake up in the morning
- How you feel arriving at work and leaving the office
- The level of respect you get at work
- The amount of pay that you receive for your efforts
- The quirks of the office that continually bother you, the lack of satisfaction

In the right-hand column, note how you would *like* to feel when you wake up and after you have completed a day's work. Write down what your dream entrepreneurial life would be like and what milestones you'd like to see as you follow your dream. Would you like to sell your product at a local craft fair or at national chain stores? Would you like to work twenty hours a week and pick up your kids at school? Would you like to secure your financial future?

The right-hand side of this list will become your goals as you begin your journey. How great would it feel to wake up early and jump out of bed with anticipation that the day can bring excitement and fulfillment? Once you have written your goals, refer back to them frequently until they become real. Rereading them, especially at difficult times, will remind you why you began this venture and what happiness may await you.

What you dislike about your current situation and the way it makes you feel	*How you would like to feel when you wake up and after you have completed a day's work*
------------------------------------	------------------------------------
------------------------------------	------------------------------------
------------------------------------	------------------------------------
------------------------------------	------------------------------------
------------------------------------	------------------------------------
------------------------------------	------------------------------------
------------------------------------	------------------------------------
------------------------------------	------------------------------------
------------------------------------	------------------------------------
------------------------------------	------------------------------------
------------------------------------	------------------------------------
------------------------------------	------------------------------------
------------------------------------	------------------------------------
------------------------------------	------------------------------------
------------------------------------	------------------------------------
------------------------------------	------------------------------------
------------------------------------	------------------------------------
------------------------------------	------------------------------------
------------------------------------	------------------------------------
------------------------------------	------------------------------------

the computer as you open the biggest purchase order you have ever seen. Envision yourself driving to the bank to deposit a check from a company you have dreamed of doing business with. Actually *feel* how it will feel.

By thinking positively, you can change how your body feels. You'll be more relaxed and focused. Just as every great golfer incorporates detailed visualization in her pre-shot routine, you must do the same for your product's game plan. While the golfer sees the ball taking the perfect flight, landing on the green at the desired spot, and rolling toward the hole, you can visualize having the perfect conversation with the buyer, receiving the purchase order, shipping your product, and seeing it on store shelves. See it, feel it.

Your heart may start beating faster when you do this positive thinking—that's because your body is responding to your adrenaline and excitement. When you encounter a difficult step in this journey, come back to these positive thoughts and re-energize yourself with them.

Commit to Perseverance

Regardless of a positive outlook, you'll no doubt encounter obstacles along the way. The key is refusing to give up when things get frustrating. Know that your journey may not be an easy one, but the rewards can last a lifetime and possibly even generations.

So don't give up when you face a problem. Commit to moving through obstacles. Commit to not taking no for an answer. Commit to the journey. Build your inner strength now so when times get tough later, you can tap into it. Your level of commitment will help separate you from those who never realize their dreams!

Feed Off of Negative Feedback

When I first started telling people that I was starting a new business designing moisturizing gloves, the response was something like, "Oh, okay. Yeah, uh . . . good luck with that. Don't quit your

If they can do it,
So Can You!

Gary Erikson's light bulb moment for his Clif bars came in the middle of a recession. But that didn't stop him because he was so tired of eating the only energy bar on the market and it was not satisfying him. He concocted his own energy bar, naming it the Clif bar after his father. By the time he shipped the first Clif bars in February 1992 that recession was officially over. Clif bar sales have since surpassed $100 million and Erikson's company will be experiencing and likely surviving its third recession in eighteen years.

day job." After my husband decided to retire from practicing law to help me run the business, you can only imagine the comments we heard. Gut instinct and intuitiveness are powerful influences from within. We chose to listen to and trust our instincts. Even after our business was earning a great income, it took about five years before people realized that we were actually successful. Those naysayers are still at their same jobs, probably wishing they had pursued their great idea. The difference between them and me: action.

Try to let people's negativity or insensitive comments fuel your desire to succeed. (Note: No "friends and family discount" for them!) Turn the negative energy into motivation and action (not in a vengeful sense, but in a "they will see" sort of way). Though it's easier said than done, find a technique that allows you to let the negative comments roll right off your back and makes you want to prove yourself that much more. It can be a "mantra" or perhaps that visualization discussed earlier. A mantra is a positive repetition of words that helps you focus and has a calming effect. It can be something as simple as a favorite quote or even a single energy-infusing word like "persistence" or "action." Repeat your mantra silently or aloud every time you hear a negative comment to find that inner strength you need to move ahead with even more steam!

Remember, negative comments are inevitable. Even when you're a success, you'll *still* get them. But rather than internalizing that negative energy, mentally convert it to fuel for your inner fire.

Find the Time

Let me guess. You're a busy person with a job, responsibility for others—younger or older, hobbies, and a social life. How will you ever find time to make your idea a reality? There's no magic answer—you just have to learn to manage your time more effectively.

Change How You Spend Your Free Time

You've probably heard the saying, "If you want something done, give it to the busiest person you know." This adage seems to hold true in so many aspects of life. Take the Parent Teacher Association at any given school. It seems to be the mom with five kids who is volunteering to help and the mom with one kid and no outside job who doesn't help much (but will still complain about the way things are done). If they're so swamped, why can busy people get more accomplished? It's usually because they already have an effective system for getting things done. But those who have inefficient time-management skills may find one small task daunting.

The bottom line: You can (and will) find a way to fit this product launch in your schedule if you want it badly enough. If you commit to mere minutes a day, you will make a lot of progress in just one week's time. Try to use your time as wisely as possible. For example, skip watching that hour-long drama on TV and instead research company names. Instead of checking out the sale rack at your favorite store, visit a local manufacturer to discuss packaging options. Chunks of time like that add up to hours of productivity and to tangible momentum.

Ask for Help

When your family and close friends realize that you are working on something that you are so passionate about, they may want to pitch in and help. Don't be shy about asking for some small favors so you can keep up momentum and make the most of each day.

For example, ask your kids to help prepare dinner and clear the table so you can get right to your work in the evening. If your children are too young to help, think about asking your relative or neighbor to entertain them for an hour or two a couple of days a week. When busy people who have a great idea actually make the time to follow a dream, it's inspiring and exciting to be around their energy.

Show your appreciation with a small gift or reward, a thoughtful note, or a promise of a discount when your product is on the shelves.

Ask Questions, Reach Out

The Biz Brainstorm: Who Do You Know? is a great starting point for gathering advice. Once you've gotten information from that group, look outside that list and e-mail someone you have only read about or someone whose product you like. Virtually every product has a website and contact information—these days, finding who you want to talk to isn't too difficult.

Take my experience with Carol Green as an example. Years ago, I watched an episode of *The Oprah Winfrey Show* that featured a panel of four women entrepreneurs. At this point, I had my idea but hadn't started working on it yet. The woman on the show who inspired me most was Carol Green, a beautiful model who was designing and marketing a sexy, new version of the old girdle. She had recently given birth and she still wanted to look great in clothes even after her body shape had changed. She found girdles on the market, but not a pretty and sexy one. So, she made one! Turns out, many other women had the same thought, but she actually took action on the idea. She sold her line in Neiman Marcus and many other department stores. It was a big success.

Who Do You Know?

Jot down the names of friends, friends of friends, family, friends of family, acquaintances, friends of acquaintances, neighbors, friends of neighbors (you get the idea), and *anyone* who may be able to give advice in regard to any aspect of the business.

If your list is long, divide it into categories based on what makes sense for your idea. You could break it into those who can help make time for you to work, those who are in the industry you're breaking into, those who can help you sell the product, and so forth. Before you speak to anyone, write down the questions you'd like to ask so you appear professional and serious about your plan. Ask and you may receive!

This episode really inspired me to get going on my gloves. I picked up the phone and actually called Carol Green to see if she had any advice for a beginning entrepreneur. Believe it or not, we spoke on the phone for about an hour! We had lots of fun talking about business and then she said she was going to be in Los Angeles and she would take a brief meeting with me to see if she could help me even more. We met at the Beverly Hills Hotel and we had breakfast (I could barely afford the orange juice at the time—and this was my first official business expense!). Carol was so generous and forthcoming with advice and helpful information.

Skipping out of the hotel, I went back to my "office" feeling like my business had just gotten started that day. The moral of my story: Don't be intimidated by those who are already successful. Contact them anyway! At worst, the person doesn't give you any advice. At best, you get a wealth of insider information. You just have to ask.

million-dollar TIP When meeting with a mentor, find a quiet place to talk. Don't pick restaurants where tables are very close together. You can also visit your mentor at her office first. It's probably the most convenient option for her, and you want to make this meeting easy for her. Or, ask the mentor to choose a meeting place.

Don't Worry about Money Yet

Regardless of how motivated, excited, and positive you are about your great idea, I'm sure one major question still lingers in your mind: *How will I ever pay for this?* At this early stage, consider financing your idea to be just one step in the process, not a deal breaker. I know—easy for someone else to say, right?

Yes, you will have to figure out how you'll pay for the bigger expenses that you will incur down the road, such as:

- Trademarks, patents, and other intellectual property rights
- Prototypes and samples
- Your first large manufacturing run
- Packaging materials
- Marketing and promotional materials

It doesn't cost money to research online and plan your journey to success. That is absolutely free. Begin with research and when you feel confident that your idea is on solid ground, you can think further about where you can access some money.

Most likely you will begin the journey as I did, as a "bootstrapper" —someone who starts a business without capital. Most people do not have the capital to start a business in a "big" way. On Day 1, they don't hire designers, public relations people, administrative help, and a sales force. Most entrepreneurs start out pinching pennies and handling the responsibilities of many positions on their own.

> Clear your mind, start on a positive note, and adjust your psyche. Let yourself enjoy the excitement and anticipation of what lies ahead. If you really believe that your idea will appeal to many others, or you can't seem to stop thinking about it, it's time to take a risk. Follow your dream!

bring your idea to life

All our dreams can come true, if we have the courage to pursue them.

—WALT DISNEY

Now that you know what it takes to be an entrepreneur, it's time to set your idea free. It needs to exit your head. Let the idea come alive and begin its life. Let's start by identifying what kind of idea you have.

Types of New Ideas

Many people think of product ideas frequently, simply based on their need for something newer, easier, or better. Whenever I ask someone how he or she thought of a successful product idea, the answer is usually "because I needed it." The person had a recurring problem, thought of a great solution, and then made that solution a viable product. As they say, necessity is the mother of invention. And if you have the same problem over and over, chances are good that others are struggling with it too.

Ideas for products usually fit into one of three categories: a product completely new to the marketplace, an upgrade to an already existing product, or using an existing product in a totally new way or in a new marketplace. The following sections will detail each type so you can learn which category best fits your product. This knowledge will help determine how to sell the product and differentiate it from competition.

A Brand-New Product

If you think of a completely new product that you have never seen before, you might wonder why it's not in the marketplace already. It might seem like such a simple idea that you think, "Someone must have tried to invent this product before; it's so obvious." But that may not be the case—you may be the one that has to develop it!

Liquid Paper is a good example of a brand-new product unlike anything else when it hit the market. Originally called "Mistake Out" in 1951, it was developed by a secretary named Bette Nesmith Graham. Liquid Paper was her own concoction used to cover up her typing mistakes. I bet other secretaries had wished for such a thing as well, but Bette took action and found a way to make correcting her mistakes easier and more professional looking. She mixed batches of white tempera paint, applied it to paper, and it worked perfectly. She sold it out of her house for many years. Gillette bought the company from Graham in 1968 for $47.5 million plus royalties. She wasn't a scientist; she was an everyday problem solver.

If they can do it, *So Can you!*

In 1960, two brothers, Tom and James Monaghan, borrowed $900 from a local bank to purchase a pizza store in Michigan called "DomiNicks." They also bought a VW Beetle car so they could make deliveries. A year later, James traded his half of the business to Tom for the VW (oops!). Tom renamed the store Domino's. Seven years later, the first Domino's franchise opened in Michigan, and the rest is history. In 1998, Tom Monaghan announced his retirement and sold 93 percent of the company for nearly a billion dollars and retained a small non-controlling percentage of the company. Today Domino's operates approximately 8,500 franchises in more than fifty-five countries.

A New Twist on an Existing Product

We all use tools or products on a daily basis and you may find yourself questioning the performance of one of them and think, "This could be so much better if. . . ." If you've got an idea like that, it's an upgrade to an already existing product.

My Moisture Jamzz Moisture Gloves are an example of an improvement or change to an existing product. Classic, white cotton gloves had been around for generations. Women wore them over their favorite moisturizers at night to help soften hands. My product is simply an upgraded and updated version of that product. My fabrics are higher quality and include spandex for better fit and comfort; our products feature original, fun designs.

Look at the first tool kit made specifically for women. It became popular very quickly and was sold in major mass-market stores. It was a simple concept: take the standard men's tool kit and make it less intimidating for women by giving it a more feminine look and soft-grip handles. This new tool kit gave women permission to feel like they, too, could be handy around the house. Tools were no longer just for men.

Sometimes it's as simple as altering an existing product by making a few changes. Give that old product a new, fresh purpose and therefore a new, fresh audience. So even if your idea offers only a small improvement or change to an already popular product, it still has great potential!

An Existing Product with a New Purpose

Your idea falls into this category if you were using a tool or product and realized that it would also work well in a completely different capacity. In this case, the product needs to be re-marketed to a new audience in new packaging, usually with a few tweaks in design to make it appealing to the different demographic.

Write It Down, Make It Real

Your idea has been swirling around your head long enough; it's time to put it on paper. When something is committed to paper, it takes on a new reality. Take a deep breath and grab your pen. Now, in a "stream of consciousness" style of writing, just jot down everything that comes into your head about your product, such as:

- What is the name of the product?

- What does the product look like (actually draw it, even a few different ways if that's possible)?

- What is its function?

- Who will use or buy it?

- Why will people want or need it?

- What materials are involved?

- Will it have sizes or colors?

- What age group or demographic will want this?

- Why is it special? Exactly how is it different from similar items?

As you write anything and everything you can think of about your product, it begins to feel more "real."

The Microplane is the perfect example of using an already existing product in a totally new way. At a spa-themed trade show, I exhibited next to a company that sold a product called the Microplane, which scrapes the dry, dead skin away from your heels. The Microplanes were selling like hotcakes. The product had been around for more than ten years already, but used in two different markets—woodworking and kitchen tools—for two distinctly different purposes. When it was first invented, it was a tool sold in hardware stores for use with woodworking projects. It was popular within that industry, both for commercial projects and weekend warrior home-improvement projects. The Microplane had a special patented design that would very finely slice wood instead of shredding or tearing, like most of the other slicing instruments.

One day, a hardware store owner's wife was making a cake and needed to zest some orange peel for the recipe. She noticed the new tool and thought it would be perfect for the job. It *was* perfect—it finely sliced the orange's skin like no other kitchen tool she'd seen. She had her husband add that function to their store catalog and it was the beginning of the Microplane becoming a household name in the kitchen industry, too.

Then, the third marketplace use came about later as someone figured out that the same tool also worked well to gently skim dead skin off dry heels. So, this tool is popular in the toolshed, the kitchen, and now the bathroom. What's next for the Microplane?

Play Devil's Advocate

Once you've completed the Biz Brainstorm: Write It Down, Make It Real, you may feel a renewed sense of excitement for your idea. Now it's time to channel that energy back into your idea—but this time to critique it.

Put the workbook down and clear your head. Take a walk, listen to music, run some errands. When you've had enough time away from it, go back and review what you wrote. Take a completely fresh look, as if it is someone else's idea. Critique it. Look for holes in logic or research. Think of possible design flaws. Jot down these new thoughts in your workbook.

If you have identified problems, do they seem manageable? With more research, brainstorming, and ingenuity, can you fix them? If so, you've done your idea a great service by improving it at this early stage. If not, take a step back and reassess.

When you're comfortable with where your idea stands, it's time to dive into some practical matters.

At this point in your journey, you may want to keep your idea to yourself. You have momentum and you don't want to be discouraged by someone who may not "get it"—your idea, your passion, your dream. You also want to keep the idea confidential because you don't want someone to steal it! It may be tough, but mum's the word at this point.

Research Your Competition

If you've made it this far, you probably know a little something about your product's competition. Now it's time to delve deeper into that search to be sure you know virtually everything.

Check Patents

Even if you haven't seen your product idea in the marketplace you need to make sure someone else hasn't already patented it. A patent holder still owns the exclusive right to make, use, or sell the invention in the United States during the full term of the patent whether or not the invention has actually made it to the marketplace. Therefore it is necessary to search relevant patents to see if your product has already been invented, discovered, or created in some form. Discovering that your "breakthrough" idea is not so "breakthrough" after all is surely disappointing. But it is much less painful to know before you've invested in it.

According to *www.uspto.gov*, the website for the U.S. Patent and Trademark Office, more than seven million patents have been issued as of early 2008. That's a *lot* of unique ideas! The purpose of this search is to be sure your idea can be the next one assigned a patent. Don't falsely convince yourself that you have a unique product or idea only to be blindsided later, either by seeing your idea in the marketplace or, worse yet, by a lawsuit.

To begin, visit *www.uspto.gov* and search their patent database by entering keywords that describe your product. Use specific keywords, but don't conduct so narrow a search that you might miss related products. When you click on a particular product, the website will show you who owns that patent, when it was filed, and *exactly* what was patented. The descriptions are sometimes quite lengthy, as they need to clearly separate one patent from another. The site will even show images that describe how the product works. Another website that has a patent resource is *www.google.com/patents*. Be aware that there are critical time requirements for filing patent applications in certain circumstances. For this reason alone it may be worth the money to consult a patent attorney sooner rather than later.

As you review your competition's patents, really think about the little nuances that make your product more valuable and different.

Research

Once you've discovered what patents exist for products like yours, it's time to learn more about the other products, companies, and sales outlets within your industry. You should look at competitive products, newspapers (for industry or new product news), trade magazines (for industry news), and any other relevant sources.

Read your competition's sales pitch, consumer reviews, and product specifications. Then search for articles about your particular industry. Be sure you know how the industry typically fares in different economies, where its products sell best, and which products and companies are the most successful and long-running. This information will help you frame your product properly within its larger industry and learn from others' failures.

If they can do it, *So Can you!*

Jibbitz are those little personalized charms that people use to customize their Crocs shoes (or these days, any one of the imitation Crocs shoes). Sheri Schmelzer, who created Jibbitz, had three kids who wore Crocs. She had trouble differentiating whose Crocs were whose, so she made little charms (now called Jibbitz), such as soccer balls and flowers, then punched them into the holes in her kids' Crocs. Her husband had a light bulb moment when he saw these customized Crocs. Sheri began selling them in August 2005, and by September 2006, Jibbitz was grossing $2 million a month and selling in more than 4,000 stores internationally. In October 2006, Crocs bought Jibbitz for $20 million. Talk about an overnight success!

Visit stores large and small, inexpensive and expensive, near and far, and study your competition. Go in with an open mind. Make sure your product will be better, faster, more unique, an improvement, an upgrade, whatever! Basically, you want yours to be the better choice for the buying public.

Look at the way similar products are packaged and marketed, and study the lingo that is used on the packaging. Figure out who they have been marketing to (men? women? bargain shoppers? etc.) and who you will be marketing to based on the differences that you will be offering. Get into the marketplace and touch and feel, look, listen, and observe.

Compile What You've Learned

After your patent hunt, online search, and store visits, you will know
a vast amount about your product's potential. However, if you find
that your search has raised more questions, continue both online and
physical research until you are an expert on your product and how it
differs from every other item that could be considered its competitor.

You're Not Done Yet

This is not a one-stop-and-you're-done process—keep researching until you have a clear understanding of the industry as a whole.
Even after your product is released, you should stay aware of new
competition and changes in the industry. At all times, you should
know the following:

1. One or two main benefits of your product. This could be
   the solution it offers or the effect it has on customers.
2. What the consumer expects from the type of products in
   this arena. For example, if your product is a new makeup
   line for teen girls, you would need to know that they are
   interested in products that don't clog their pores or make
   their skin feel oily. You would know that they want to look
   clean and fresh, as opposed to a woman in her forties, who
   is probably more concerned about the anti-aging properties
   of her makeup.
3. The main lingo of products within that genre. For example,
   take cars. The common lingo associated with selling cars
   has to do with (in today's market) value, gas mileage, and
   the feeling that the driver gets when behind the wheel.
4. The price range for similar products. If your price range is
   very different, you need to be able to clearly explain in your
   marketing materials why yours is worth more or is much
   more affordable.
5. That you feel 100 percent confident that you have put
   together the best possible version of your product (for now).

If you can do these things, you know how to point out the assets of your product as compared to its competition. Be confident that your product is either an improvement on a product already proven in the marketplace, or that it's a product that nicely fills a void in the marketplace. Today more than ever people are looking for value, so try to offer as many benefits as possible.

While you are visiting stores, compare a few competing products of any item within the same category as your product and see how they differentiate themselves from each other. This exercise will help you learn some small, subtle ways to separate your product from the competition. This will also help you see what differences take the product to a new and higher price point.

What If I Found Something Unexpected?

Once you've checked both online and in the marketplace to see that your idea is unique, feel free to move full steam ahead. But what if your search found a product you didn't know about or a feature your product must have but currently doesn't? This is a common hurdle, so don't worry. You may just need to tweak your idea based on your findings. Simply focus on the issue and brainstorm solutions. Reread your Biz Brainstorm: Write It Down, Make It Real (see page 22) notes in your workbook and update sections as necessary based on your findings.

Stand Out from the Pack

Now that you've compiled and assessed your research, it's time to home in on what makes your product special. Most likely, your idea is not in the "brand-new product" category we identified earlier and therefore, it will need to stand out from the competition. You see examples of this all the time, whether you realize it or not. For example, a new lip gloss will generate lots of buzz within the beauty industry, even though the marketplace is already saturated with lip glosses. But the new product found a way to stand out, and if it offers even just one new, unique purpose it can become the new, hot product.

So, as you develop your idea, focus on how it will be different. Keep asking yourself the question that you will be asked frequently by your customers: "How is your product different or better than the others already out there?" We'll look further at this in Step 7.

If they can do it, *So Can You!*

Burt's Bees (a very popular line of personal care products made from beeswax) had quite a long trip from humble beginning to household name. Burt Shavitz sold quarts of honey from the back of his pickup truck while living in an 8' × 8' cabin in New England. In 1984, his friend, Roxanne Quimby, saw the leftover beeswax from Burt's honey production and decided they should make candles and sell them at a local craft fair. The by-product of his honey became the main product for their candles. They earned $200 on their first batch, and by the end of the first year, sales were up to $20,000. They decided to expand into natural soaps and lip balm, and that success led to an even larger line of all-natural bath and body products. In 1998, they had annual sales of $8 million and their Burt's Bees line was sold in more than 4,000 outlets. By 2007, their products were sold in 30,000 international retail outlets.

Choosing a Name for Your Company and/or Product

Now that you've researched the competition and thought more about how your product is different from other comparable products, it's time to finalize the name of your product. As you can imagine, this step is very important. Make a list of several names, since it is highly likely that your first choice is already taken. As you begin to think of names for the company and/or product, keep in mind:

- Try to make the spelling easy or distinctive. Moisture Jamzz has been sometimes difficult with the two zs at the end. However, people remember the name—and that's the important part.
- Consider whether or not you want to be the face of the company. If I develop a new soap and call it Sandy's Organic Soaps, I would have to be ready and willing to promote myself and be a great representative of the line. Or you can use a generic "face" for the company, such as Mama's Pasta Sauce or Sweetie's Baby Shampoo. This way the product feels "homemade" but you are not the "model."
- Be sure the name isn't a common word in a foreign language like Spanish or French—languages that many Americans know pretty well. Remember the Chevrolet car named "Nova"? I remember hearing the joke about its name because in Spanish it translates to "No go." Not a great name for a car! So, you need to do a little research before you set it all in stone.

In order to see if anyone else has taken the name you want, again visit *www.uspto.gov*, but this time, click on "trademarks" and search that database for similar names. The search should pull up both "live" (currently held) and "dead" (those that have expired) trademarks using the keywords you provide. The site will also tell you the industry associated with a particular trademark, along with relevant images. (We'll talk more about protecting and trademarking your name in Step 4.)

Trust Your Inner Voice

As you progress on your journey, you will have to make lots of decisions. It's a process like building a home from scratch—you have to decide on everything from the shape of the house down to the last drawer handle. You may not immediately know the "right" answers because you have never been in this position before. Although you may feel overwhelmed by so many decisions, make them mindfully and take your time. Be patient and think over the options carefully.

It might be tempting to make a quick decision to keep yourself moving, but allow yourself time to ponder and consider pros and cons of the different choices. Trust your gut instinct, but question it before making a final decision on new and/or important issues. Remember, you can always ask someone who has experience for advice. As you get deeper into the process, your knowledge base will widen and you will gain more confidence with each decision.

Now you are at a point where you have done your research and your idea is coming to fruition. You are on your way to producing a product that you are passionate about and you are willing to go the distance. Take a deep breath and move ahead with confidence, patience, inner strength, persistence, and determination. Next step!

STEP
3

bootstrapping: make the most of your own resources

By not risking anything, you risk more.
—ERICA JONG

You're going to think I'm crazy, but it's true: Don't let the fact that you may have little or no money stop you from getting your product into the marketplace. If every entrepreneur let money be an obstacle, we wouldn't have many of our favorite products. At this point in your journey, you need to start spending some money. (At first, it's to protect the intellectual property rights of your product—more about this in Step 4.) Do not get overwhelmed if you lack money. You just need to be aware of your financial situation and do the best you can with what you've got. Today's economy really doesn't change the financial issue for many entrepreneurs, as the cold hard truth is that obtaining a bank loan even in a great economy is difficult for many beginning entrepreneurs without deep pockets. You can "blame" it on the economy and move forward in good company with those of us who started with nothing and somehow found our way, little by little.

I am not a financial expert and am not advising you as such in this chapter, but I will review the most basic and simple financial options available to you. I'll assume that you don't have deep pockets. Keep in mind that it is possible to build a business on a shoestring budget. You will find that you need money in stages, but it's important to get a sense of the total amount you'll need. To begin getting your mind around how much money you'll need, list all the things that will cost some money. (See Biz Brainstorm: List Initial Expenses for Your Budget, on page 36.) Also, consider out-of-the-box ways to follow your dream in phases—that option may reduce costs. For example, if you have a product that is inexpensive to produce and does not require a patent, you will probably not have to go into deep debt just to sell from a sample or prototype. Many people attend trade shows with only a few samples of their product. This is a great way to avoid "scary" debt before getting feedback from legitimate buyers in your industry.

The Good News

Though you may feel that you're the only entrepreneur without millions of dollars in start-up capital (or even thousands of dollars), you are not in a unique situation—quite the opposite, actually.

The good news about that situation? Business analysts have said that it doesn't always matter how much money you start with. On *Inc.* magazine's 2002 Top 500 list, amount of start-up capital was not the leading predictor of success. Companies launched with less than $1,000 were as likely to be profitable as those started with more than $100,000. It's more important that a person have the ability to manage, run, and grow a business.

Dealing with Debt

Unfortunately, for most of us, going into debt is part of the reality of bringing a product to market. But try not to fear debt. Most people are in debt at some point in their lives—from owning a car or home or going to college. Here are some ways to come to terms with your debt.

Have a Healthy Mindset

For bootstrapping entrepreneurs today, I would adjust that old adage from "it takes money to make money" to "it takes debt to make money." What I mean is: It's part of the process for most entrepreneurs. The key is to be so genuinely passionate about your product idea that you won't lose sleep at night because of the amount of debt accrued on your credit cards and/or from loans (probably from friends and family). Consider it a part of the process—just like finding a name, filing a patent, making a prototype, and so on.

Think of it like a student who takes on loans to pay for college. Many people feel that their student loan debt is the cost of ensuring their future. They are comfortable with taking on debt for the purpose of education, because that degree will help them find a job, or make more money, or do whatever it is they're trying to do. They look at the debt as an inevitable responsibility that paves the way for them to be successful in life. Try to adopt this mindset about your business debt as you push the product along toward success.

If they can do it, So Can you!

You may not know the name Fred DeLuca, but you probably have eaten one of his sandwiches. Fred DeLuca started Subway in 1965 to earn money for college. A family friend lent him $2,000, which he used to rent a storefront (without signing a lease), and buy a specific sink he needed. He set up shop with what he had. Still, he found a way to move forward on a tiny budget. Most importantly, he believed in sandwiches, which had special meaning to him. As a young kid, his family's Sunday treat was a trip to an Italian deli. So, he followed his passion. Today there are more than 28,000 Subways in eighty-six countries and it is still a privately held company with DeLuca's net worth said to be over a billion dollars, making him one of *Forbes'* richest Americans.

List Initial Expenses for Your Budget

Get your workbook out again and make an itemized list of your projected operating expenses. You may not know exact dollar amounts yet, but ballpark it and add them to the list. As you progress through the book and gain more knowledge of what your product needs, fill in those costs too. Your initial list could include such things as:

Office	
Business phone/Internet connection	
P.O. box	
Desk supplies	
Computer	
Marketing materials	
Design of logo, fliers, brochures, etc.	
Printing costs	

Mailing costs	
Photographer charges for product images	
Website consultant fees	
Research and development	
Consulting fees for a lawyer about trademarks	
Corporation filing fees	
Checking account setup fees	
Costs for a trade-show booth	
Production costs	
Product mockup and prototype expenses	
Initial production-run charges	
Storage or warehouse fees	

Look to the Future

If you are willing and able to take the risk of debt, it could be the beginning of financial success and independence. As your product becomes profitable, you can pay off debt and build real savings. Accept debt, and use your funds intelligently to get the most "bang for the buck." You'll learn to manage your debt and your eventual cash flow to keep yourself afloat. It's important to prioritize your expenses. You can't do everything you will want to do, so make "wish lists" and spend your money on things in order of importance.

Using Credit Cards

You may have imagined walking into your local bank, telling the loan officer all about your great idea, and having him happily hand over every cent you'll need to finance your venture. Well, sorry to burst your bubble, but that's usually not how it goes. Most bootstrapping entrepreneurs turn to credit cards to get their businesses off the ground. You're no doubt familiar with how credit cards work; for your business, the risks and benefits are no different.

How to Get Credit Cards in a Tough Economy

When the economy is slow, the credit card industry suffers along with everyone else. The economic crisis of 2008 had a particularly significant impact on lines of credit. With the precarious situation of credit card companies, you may be given a smaller credit limit than in previous years and the interest rate may be higher. Also, keep in mind that your interest rate can change at any time ("at the bank's sole discretion," as the fine print reads) so keep a close eye on your monthly statements. In years past, if you maxed out one credit card, you waited until you received another credit card offer in the mail and opened another account. Today, forget about it—those mailers are not coming. Banks are not offering that same credit line. No matter what the economy, your best bet for a good deal is to keep your credit rating as high as possible by paying all your bills on time.

Pros of Using Credit Cards

The main benefit of using credit cards to finance your venture is simply that it's the easiest money to obtain. They're easy to use, and are sometimes your *only* choice. Even with the credit crisis, they are readily available and, unlike investors or family members, they don't ask questions.

Credit cards are helpful for tax purposes as well. You have a record of your business expenses on your statement for tax write offs/deductions. In fact American Express Business cards generally will send you a quarterly breakdown of your charges so that you can analyze your expenses and have the list handy for your accountant. You never want to pay cash for a business expense; always have a record of the transaction. Your accountant will explain which expenses are tax deductible and can be used to offset losses on your annual tax return.

Cons of Using Credit Cards

Credit card usage can become a slippery slope, so you do need to be careful. Here are two major pitfalls.

1. **High interest rates.** The costs associated with high interest rates add up quickly, especially if you regularly only pay the small monthly amount due. You can get away with paying the small monthly amount due for only a few months— after that, you need to pay more if you want to chip away at the growing debt. If you charge a lot on the credit card and don't pay more than the minimum due every month, each subsequent charge will actually cost you a lot more than the original amount you charged. This is because you are paying the high interest rate on the accumulation of your unpaid balance. Multiply every purchase by your inter-est rate, add on that amount, and that's what you're *really* paying.

How to Save on Living Expenses

Saving money at home will augment any money you secure through other methods. Get out your workbook and make a list of ways that you are willing to save money. Divide the list into things you can give up daily, weekly, monthly, or yearly. Really think about ways you can save; small amounts add up.

DAILY

WEEKLY

MONTHLY

YEARLY

---

2. **Thinking that a credit limit equals cash.** When you see the "credit limit" amount on your statement, it can feel like a real cash infusion, but don't be fooled. Credit card limits *cannot* be considered income. Spend that amount as carefully as you would spend hard-earned money.

As you probably know from personal use, credit card purchases add up quickly. Think about each purchase before you make it. Don't be impulsive, be frugal. And be frugal but not cheap! Spend what you need to make your product viable in the marketplace.

Loans from Family and Friends

If the risks of credit card debt make you nervous, you may want to see if you can get an interest-free loan from family or friends.

Get It in Writing

Even if you have a close relationship with the lender, you probably want to have this I.O.U. in writing. That way, expectations are clearly stated and both parties are on the same page. In the I.O.U., establish the following:

1. **How long before you have to pay them back.** Ask for at least eighteen months. Bringing a product to market takes time and you don't need the added pressure of a fast-approaching family-imposed deadline.
2. **An interest rate (if applicable).** If the person insists that you pay interest (grovel first!), you need to agree on an interest rate. Refer to local banks for an average savings account interest rate, but of course, try to get yourself a better deal! (A note: Even if you have to pay interest, consider yourself lucky that you didn't give away a piece of business ownership to get it. It is much better to take on debt than give up a piece of your pie at this early stage. Your business cannot

be fairly valued at this point so you would blindly be giving up a percentage of your profits.)

3. **Penalties if you miss the due date.** Could the person extend the loan if you notify them at the nine- or ten-month mark? Even if you plan to pay on time, have a discussion about their expectations. If they can't afford to extend the loan or if you are not completely comfortable that you will be in a position to pay it back, think twice about accepting. (Check with a more distant relative with whom you wouldn't mind losing your relationship. Just kidding!) Though you obviously don't want to default on this loan, try to find someone who would not be adversely affected if you never paid them back. The lender should be comfortable going into the loan process knowing that you offer no guarantees.

4. **The form of written agreement that needs to be completed for everyone to be comfortable.** An I.O.U. is an informal agreement and acknowledgment for a small loan. It can be either verbal or written and is used when a formal contract may feel too "official" for family or close friends. A legal I.O.U. is called a promissory note. It is legally binding and can be used in court. You can find a sample Unsecured Promissory Note on the U.S. Chamber of Commerce's website: *www.uschamber.com.*

Remember, you don't need to offer your lender a piece of the business. You simply need to borrow some money. It's also useful if the person has no stipulations on what the money be spent on, so long as it's related to your idea. (You may want to pay off some credit card debt with the loan, for example.)

The Emotional Side

David Deeds, an assistant professor of entrepreneurship at Case Western Reserve University in Cleveland says borrowing money from family members is, "The highest risk money you'll ever get.

The venture may succeed or fail, but either way, you still have to go to Thanksgiving dinner." This is funny, but true. You want to find family and/or friends who want to invest in you and your product because they believe in you and feel you are competent and likely to succeed. You don't want to have to talk business and show your accounting books every time you attend a family function. Choosing a lender is very important and should be considered on these emotional levels, too.

If they can do it, *So Can You!*

Mark and Stacy Andrus pinched pennies and lived a frugal lifestyle to put everything they had into their Stacy's Pita Chips business, which started as a sandwich cart in Boston in 1997. The cart was so popular that when long lines were forming at lunchtime, they gave customers their homemade pita chips to keep them happy while they waited. In 1998, they gave up the cart and took a leap of faith—they moved into a building to manufacture the wildly popular Stacy's Pita Chips. They bought used equipment, drove old cars, and cut pitas by hand until they knew they could afford automation. As of 2001, they had $370,000 in bank and federal loans to operate their business, which became profitable that year. They acquired large chain-store accounts and began to private label their chips for Trader Joe's. PepsiCo. bought Stacy's Pita Chips in 2005 as sales approached $60 million.

Utilizing Your Bank

Though business lending is extremely tough to come by, don't ignore your local bank's options. For example, if you have a good relationship with your bank, when you open your business checking account you will likely be able to have a credit card issued in your business name and have it guaranteed by your personal bank account. This one credit card may offer you enough spending room to get your product to market if you have an inexpensive product to produce and you spend wisely.

Your bank probably has other programs you should check out as well.

Bank Loans

Don't kill the messenger, but in a tough economy, unless you have a very strong history with your bank, a pristine credit history, and a high credit rating, it is unlikely that you will be offered a loan in the start-up phase of the business. Ask the loan officer what you can do to increase your chances of getting the loan. For example, one option might be to have a relative who is financially secure cosign a loan with you.

As they say, the best time to apply for a bank loan or line of credit is when you don't need it. Once you are in the black and have some income in the bank, apply for a line of credit. Believe me, it will come in handy. Business is cyclical and you will likely find you need the extra money at some point.

Small Business Administration

Another resource for small business funding is the U.S. Small Business Administration (SBA), *www.sba.gov*. This governmental agency was established to help small businesses in many different ways. The SBA's basic 7(a) loan is their primary small business loan program. It allows the loan to be funded for a variety of purposes, such as "working capital, machinery and equipment, furniture and fixtures, land and building (including purchase, renovation, and new construction), leasehold improvements, and debt refinancing (under special conditions)."

It is a great program, but in today's economy, the money is not coming freely. Many small businesses are finding it almost impossible to get approval for even SBA loans. The demand for small business loans is far exceeding the supply available, and the credit risk for small businesses is just too high. Contrary to what many believe, the SBA does not make direct loans—they work through traditional banks or lenders (and therefore are feeling the crunch too). The SBA is thereby able to provide financing to qualified applicants by guaranteeing a portion of the loan for the bank, but the bank assumes the rest of the risk.

 The SBA has a partnership with an organization called SCORE (Service Corp. of Retired Executives). SCORE allows you to connect with executives who volunteer their time to advise start-up entrepreneurs. Visit their website at *www.score.org.*

Investors

Angel investors may seem like a gift from heaven when you have exhausted all of your other potential sources for money. Angel investors are usually wealthy persons who invest money into a start-up, looking for big returns. Their interest is in small businesses with huge growth potential. They are often willing to invest a larger sum of money than what can be collected from friends and family, typically ranging from $300,000 to $5 million. It can be a win-win scenario—she has money to invest; you need money to spend! But as with any lending arrangement, there are caveats.

The Catch: They Usually Want Partial Ownership

In exchange for their investment, angel investors typically demand an equity stake in the business, ranging from 10 to 50 percent. You will have to decide whether or not you are willing to give up partial (or possibly even *complete*) control of your company in exchange for the money. Some angel investors may offer an interest-bearing loan with no ownership equity but they will still usually insist on some input or management control of the business as well as a high interest rate.

Angel investors fund both start-ups and established small businesses in need of cash for one reason or another. For example, a growing company may need a loan to fund production for a large order or to pay for a major marketing program.

Where Are These Angels?

Angel investors are not easy to find, and you need to make a good match with one, so know that finding one can be a lengthy and complex process. Today, there are both individual angels and angel networks or groups where these investors pool their investments. Begin your search by asking for referrals from:

- **Your accountant:** Accountants usually have networks and resources to find investors.
- **Your attorney:** Start by asking your trademark lawyer. If he doesn't know of anyone, ask him to query other attorneys in his office, which may be very large and a good referral network.
- **Business magazines:** Try *Inc.*, *Entrepreneur*, and *Fortune Small Business*. See if you can find articles about other small businesses that have had success with angel funding—many times the angels' names are featured.
- **Your local chamber of commerce:** It may host venture capital group networking opportunities.
- **Friends and family:** You may feel like you can't ask for anything else from your family and friends, but referrals are easy. The more people who know you are looking for money, the better chance you'll find someone willing and able to help.
- **A local venture capital firm:** Touch base, explain a little bit about your situation, and ask if they know of angel networks.

- **Other entrepreneurs:** You might meet them through local business networking groups or find a blog online.
- **Your bank.**

To help incentivize people to help you, you could even offer a small finder's fee (possibly saved up from all of your penny-pinching efforts) to the person who connects you with the right match. Once you find your angel, the work begins again as you collaborate to come to terms on the vast array of details. Consult with your business attorney and accountant before entering into any legal arrangement.

You, Incorporated

Finding the cash to fund your idea won't be easy, so you'll need to ask for as little as possible in the beginning. The best way to save money on expenses early on is to do every task you possibly can yourself—even things you would absolutely hate to do if your "boss" asked you to. Put your ego aside—you are not "above" doing any job now.

Sure, it would be nice to have an assistant, a tech guru, an accounts payable person, or even an errand runner. But realistically, you'll likely wear all of those hats. You will have to take charge of virtually every position in the beginning, but you can also welcome and accept help from those who offer.

Consider utilizing the services of an intern. Interns are usually college students or recent grads who are trying to gain experience in a specific field. To get that experience, they sometimes volunteer their time or work for a minimal amount or for college credits.

When people see that you, too, are willing to do the "grunt" work without complaining, they will too. Years later, I promise that you will be happy that you experienced all of those positions as you will have a better understanding of how each person's responsibilities affect the business as a whole.

At this point, think of the glass as half full rather than half empty and know that other entrepreneurs have likely been in worse shape than you financially and have made it out of debt to become very profitable. Utilize the funds you have intelligently as you continue your journey. Where there's a will, there's a way!

STEP
4

understand legal issues

The trouble with law is lawyers.
—CLARENCE DARROW

Don't worry; I'm not going to throw a bunch of legal mumbo-jumbo at you so your eyes glaze over. (There is a reason that I did not attend law school!) But a budding entrepreneur does need to know a bare minimum about the legal issues of entrepreneurship.

First, all entrepreneurs should know the basics of "intellectual property" law as it relates to protecting their product idea. Your intellectual property (IP) attorney can explain the details pertaining to your situation, but I will touch on the basics. Second, you should become familiar with the most common forms of business ownership. You'll undoubtedly encounter other legal issues such as business insurance, taxes, and employee relations further down the road.

Just to touch on product liability insurance, you'll want to look into liability insurance before your product is available to the public. Your current homeowner's or renter's insurance agent should be able to help you secure a reasonable business liability insurance policy. Think about all the potential injuries or harm that your product could conceivably cause. The "danger or harm" level of your product will dictate the amount of liability you will need. For example if you are selling something with small parts that a child could choke on and the product is for the children's market, you will need a higher amount of liability insurance in place as your product enters the marketplace.

As a disclaimer, I am not an attorney and certainly will not dispense legal advice. But I will share what I've learned about intellectual product protection and ownership, and I hope you will find it helpful in your journey.

Intellectual Property Basics

Just as landowners have property rights to protect their land from intrusion, companies and business owners can acquire, to the extent allowed by law, certain exclusive rights to their "property." These rights are known as intellectual property (IP) rights. The term "intellectual property" refers to the entire realm of protection for inventions (patents), artistic expression copyrights, and product source identification (trademarks and trade dress). "Trade dress" is the visual characteristics of a product or service that includes such things as packaging appearance or restaurant décor that identify a source to consumers. For example, the distinctive décor of a McDonald's restaurant both inside and out would be an example of protectable trade dress because it signifies to the consumer that they are in a McDonald's. Should another restaurant copy the décor in a meaningful way, McDonald's would sue for trade dress infringement. Not only will knowing IP basics allow you to communicate more efficiently with your IP attorney, but it will also help you understand how to protect your product and respect the rights of others. Intellectual property rights (trademarks, copyrights, and patents) must be applied for and are conveyed by the U.S. government. If you don't apply for these protections in a timely fashion, you risk losing ownership and may have greater difficulty proving ownership or enforcing your rights.

Do I Really Need an IP Lawyer?

Dealing with intellectual property is an area where many inexperienced entrepreneurs with a great idea get intimidated and are tempted to cut corners. This is a very bad idea! If you ignore these legal issues now, your business can implode later with lawsuits involving trademark infringement or other legal nightmares. Patent applications are time-consuming and costly, and trademarks and copyrights can be confusing and complex; your best bet is to hire an attorney. You'll be able to move ahead with confidence that you have protected your product and not infringed on anyone else's products.

It is important to note that your IP lawyer—not you—will be responsible for meeting all the filing deadlines. A single missed deadline can result in your intellectual property being unprotected and vulnerable to theft. Most IP offices have an elaborate calendaring system that tracks thousands of deadlines for their clients' applications and registrations. You have other things to worry about!

If they can do it, *So Can You!*

There are two fewer lawyers practicing today since Rick Rosenfield and Larry Flax left the legal jungle for the pizza industry in 1985. They reinvented pizza by using exotic flavors from around the world and opened their California Pizza Kitchen restaurant in Beverly Hills. The chain today operates, licenses, or franchises more than 240 California Pizza Kitchen restaurants in thirty-three states and eight foreign countries. They also have a line of frozen foods with Kraft foods. Yes, they were lawyers, not chefs. But it goes to show that if you have a great idea, run with it; your background doesn't matter.

How Do I Find a Reputable IP Lawyer?

The best way to find a good IP attorney is by word of mouth. Ask family, friends, or any experienced lawyer you may know for a referral. Try the website *www.martindale.com*—it lists all practicing lawyers by state. It has a vast database of attorneys you can search by name, specialty, or geographic area, and it lists most attorneys' credentials and experience.

Budgeting for Your IP Attorney

Whereas personal injury lawyers generally work on a contingency fee, nearly all IP lawyers work strictly on an hourly basis. They usually require an initial retainer and will bill you by the quarter hour (or other fraction). Before hiring your IP lawyer, find out how they charge their time so there's no big surprises on your bill. Hourly rates for attorneys differ according to their city and whether they work for a large or smaller firm. One way to cut costs here is to work with a junior partner or associate, whose hourly rate is much less than that of a senior attorney. Consider a junior partner or associate if your idea is straightforward, easily explained, and not too similar to other products or services in existence. Also, most IP lawyers will allow you a free initial consultation. It never hurts to ask.

Some IP lawyers will charge on a flat-fee basis for more routine trademark and copyright filings. For example, lawyers usually charge $1,200 to $1,500 to file a trademark application, including the existing trademark search and government filing fee ($350 per class of goods or services per online application at this time). They may give you a break when more than one application needs to be filed. They may charge artwork fees if necessary for the application.

Before you meet with a lawyer, it's important to learn some basics about intellectual property so you have an idea of what you need.

Types of Intellectual Property

A broad overview of the main types of intellectual property can be found in the table on the facing page.

PROPERTY RIGHT	PROTECTS	TERM	EXAMPLES
PATENTS	Inventions		
Utility Patents	Useful processes, machines, manu-factured items, and compositions		Wind turbines, medicine
Design Patents	Original, orna-mental designs for manufactured items	20 years	The look of an athletic shoe, bicycle helmet, action figure
Plant Patents	Invented or dis-covered asexually reproduced plant varieties		Hybrid tea roses, Silver Queen Corn
TRADEMARKS	Words, names, symbols, sounds, or colors that dis-tinguish goods and services	Can be renewed for-ever (with continued use)	The roar of the MGM lion, the shape of the Coca-Cola bottle, the name "Coke"
COPYRIGHTS	Protects works of authorship such as writings, music, and works of art tangibly expressed	Lasts for the life of the author plus 70 years	*Gone with the Wind* (book and film), video games
TRADE SECRETS	Information that companies keep secret that gives them a competitive advantage.	Trade secrets are not formally registered with any governmen-tal agency; there is no term or expira-tion associated with them. That is, trade secrets remain pro-tectable as long as they remain secret. In situations where there is theft of trade secrets or the pos-sibility of employees divulging a compa-ny's trade secrets the company must seek relief from the appropriate court.	The formula for Coca-Cola

Source: www.uspto.gov

Do I Need a Patent, Trademark, or Copyright Protection?

Patents, trademarks, and copyrights each cover a distinct aspect of "property" protection. Many people (understandably) confuse the three. Let's start with a quick multiple-choice quiz using some basic examples to test your level of knowledge on the differences.

Pop Quiz

1. You design a piece of artwork that you want to print on T-shirts. To protect the artwork do you need to apply for a trademark, copyright, and/or patent?
2. You name your new company Mary's Marvelous Cookies. To protect the name should you apply for a patent, copyright, or trademark?
3. You invent the perfect new tool to use in place of the standard "whatever" tool that's on the market. To protect your new tool, should you apply for a patent, trademark, or copyright?

Short Answers

1. Copyright and/or trademark (see, it can be complicated!)
2. Trademark
3. Patent

As you can see, the answers may not be as cut-and-dried as you think. These complications make it essential to see an IP attorney in the beginning stages for some education and direction.

million-dollar TIP

Trade secrets, while not registered the same way as patents, trademarks, and copyrights, are still protected by law. In 2006, three people were arrested for allegedly selling trade secret information of Coca-Cola to PepsiCo. for $1.5 million. The FBI conducted an undercover sting, which led to the arrests of these three people, one of whom was a Coca-Cola employee. "Information is the lifeblood of a company," said Coca-Cola CEO Neville Isdell.

You may run into special situations depending on who's helping you at various stages. Let's say someone else designed the artwork for you in question #1. Who owns the work? Since technically the person who created the art owns it, if you hire someone to create artwork, you need that person to formally transfer ownership of the design to you in writing using an "assignment." You can find sample copyright assignment forms online (visit *www.copylaw.com*) or at the library that you can modify, or hire an attorney to draft one for your specific situation. The moral of the story: Use an IP lawyer—don't guess or take chances.

Patents

A patent is an exclusive right given by a government to the inventor of a product or process for a certain period of time, depending on the type of patent. During the protected period of time, the patent owner can prevent others from making, using, or selling the invention within the issuing country. Patents are granted for inventions or discoveries of new and useful items, and are also granted for the improvement of existing inventions. For example, the inventor of a new type of can opener can receive a patent as well as someone who invents a new and useful improvement to an existing can opener. Within the category of patents, there are different types, such as a design, utility, and plant.

Since the rights granted by a United States patent extend only throughout the territory of the United States and have no effect in a foreign country, an inventor who wishes patent protection in other countries must apply for a patent in each of the other countries or in regional patent offices. Almost every country has its own patent law, and a person desiring a patent in a particular country must make an application for a patent in that country, in accordance with the requirements of that country.

Excerpted from General Information Concerning Patents print brochure and found on the *uspto.gov* website in the treaties section.

How Do I Get a Patent?

In the United States, patents are granted by the U.S. Patent and Trademark Office. You must use a lawyer for this process—the U.S. government will not accept applications from non-attorneys due to the rigorous specifications. The attorneys' fees and application costs can run into the tens of thousands of dollars, depending on the complexity of your invention and the number of times the Patent Office and your attorney have to communicate (sometimes the Patent Office needs to ask clarifying questions or requests more material or explanation).

Should I Apply for a Patent?

The best way to find out if you should apply for a patent is to contact a patent attorney. But you can first read about the different types of patents on *www.uspto.gov* so you have some background. When in doubt, protect yourself and your product, and have your patent attorney apply for one.

When Should I Apply for a Patent?

As an entrepreneur with a product idea that may be patentable, be aware that there is a critical deadline for filing your patent application that has to do with the first time you make your invention "public." United States patent law provides for a one-year "grace period" for filing a patent application from the date the invention is "made public." Also referred to as the "on-sale bar rule," this rule states that an invention is not eligible for patent if the invention was patented or described in a printed publication in this or a foreign country or in public use or on sale in this country, more than one year prior to the date of application for patent in the United States.

Search Existing Patents

Obviously, it will save you a lot of time and money if you find out your invention is ineligible for patent protection before meeting with an attorney. You can easily search existing patents and educate yourself on the patent process by visiting *www.uspto.gov*. Another website that has a patent resource is *www.google.com/patents*. Be aware that there are critical time requirements for filing patent applications in certain circumstances. For this reason alone it may be well worth the money to consult with a patent attorney sooner rather than later.

million-dollar TIP Not every product idea needs to go through the lengthy and costly process of obtaining a utility patent. Hallelujah! Check with your IP attorney to see if you can get enough protection from trademarks, copyrights, or a less expensive design patent.

Trademarks

According to the U.S. Patent and Trademark Office, a trademark is "a word, name, symbol, or device that is used in trade with goods to indicate the source of the goods and to distinguish them from the goods of others. A service mark is the same as a trademark except that it identifies and distinguishes the source of a service rather than a product."

Acme Cleaners has a service mark, as they provide a service, where as Coca-Cola has a trademark, since it's a product.

Although limited trademark rights theoretically exist without a formal registration, don't chance it. Meaningful countrywide protection is only granted by the Patent and Trademark Office, via an application process.

Do I Need an Attorney?

Unlike a patent, the government allows non-attorneys to file for trademark registrations either through the mail or online at *www .uspto.gov*. Although filing on your own will save you money, it could cost you in other ways. Trademark attorneys are experts in reviewing existing trademarks, filing the application, and dealing with the Trademark Office examiners who will be reviewing your application. A trademark attorney will also help you develop a general trademark strategy—what to apply for now, what to plan for in the future, and so on. When an entrepreneur does not have the luxury of patent protection for his product, whether because the product idea is not patentable, deemed too costly a process, or some other reason, trademark protection becomes all the more critical in the marketing success of the product. Since the entrepreneur cannot legally keep competitors from "knocking-off" the product, he must rely on his trademark or brand name to maintain an advantage over competitors.

Copyrights

According to *www.uspto.gov,* a copyright is a form of protection provided to the authors of "original works of authorship," including literary, dramatic, musical, artistic, and certain other intellectual works, both published and unpublished. While inventions are matters for patent protection, copyright protection covers the *expression* of ideas. Copyrights do not protect ideas alone, methods, or systems. The distinction is confusing, but important.

Ideas vs. the Expression of Ideas

My husband, Ron, an attorney who has a lot of experience with trademark issues, is frequently approached by people with "great ideas" for something. He tells them, "Ideas are not protectable. Only the *expression* of those ideas in the form of songs, books, or artwork is protectable."

Is your head spinning? (I told you, get a lawyer!) Here's how the Patent and Trademark Office explains the difference (see box on facing page).

Copyright protection extends to a description, explanation, or illustration of an idea or system, assuming that the requirements of the copyright law are met. Copyright in such a case protects the particular literary or pictorial expression chosen by the author. However, it gives the copyright owner no exclusive rights in the idea, method, or system involved.

Suppose, for example, that an author writes a book explaining a new system for food processing. The copyright of the book, which comes into effect at the moment the work is fixed in a tangible form, will prevent others from publishing the text and illustrations describing the author's ideas for machinery, processes, and merchandising methods. But it will not give the author any rights to prevent others from adopting the ideas for commercial purposes or from developing or using the machinery, processes, or methods described in the book.—*Circular 31, Ideas, Methods, or Systems*, U.S. Copyright Office

Therefore, if you have a great idea that is not patentable, once you blurt it out to the world you basically cannot stop someone from using your idea. If something is not patentable it could be because someone has already patented it or it is deemed "obvious" or perhaps past the "one-year grace period."

How Do I Get Copyright Protection?

Copyright applications are filed with the Copyright Office, which is part of the Library of Congress. Applications can be filed by non-attorneys, and the fee is $45 at this time ($35 if you submit it online) for most copyrights. Visit *www.copyright.gov* to familiarize yourself with the various copyright forms and requirements. Unlike patents or trademarks, the Copyright Office does not perform a search of prior records. Patent and trademark attorneys will usually handle copyright applications as well. But because there are no general databases of previously copyrighted materials, the application process is very straightforward.

Monitoring Your Trademark Rights

Once you receive a trademark you will no doubt receive a solicitation from one or more trademark monitoring services (also called trademark watching services). For a fee, these companies will monitor trademark filings made in the United States and around the world, and alert you to any similar filings.

The oldest and best-known monitoring service is called Thomson Compumark. *(http://compumark.thomson.com/do/pid/107)*. Speak with your IP lawyer about whether a monitoring service is right for you and your budget. It is a great way to nip possible infringement disputes in the bud, since you will be able to confront the potential infringer in most cases before they can impact your product.

Whether or not you use a monitoring service, it's important to keep your eyes and ears open for any infringements of your IP rights. If you see something questionable in a store or are told about a confusingly similar product to yours (a friend says "I saw your product in Macy's," but your product is not sold there), investigate promptly and contact your IP attorney, who will help you formulate the best strategy for dealing with it.

There are also patent monitoring services that will alert you to new patent filings related to your patent or industry. Such a service is useful in keeping abreast of what your competition is doing and may also provide you with new licensing opportunities based on new filings. One such company providing this service is IPX *(www.ipxonline.com)*.

Moving Forward

Now that you've learned what your product needs, it's time to meet with your IP attorney. Because IP attorneys charge on an hourly basis, be prepared for your initial meeting.

Be sure you've completed the following tasks.

Checklist to Follow Prior to Meeting with Your IP Attorney

○ Could you briefly explain the basic differences between patents, trademarks, and copyrights? This will demonstrate to the attorney that you've done your homework and he won't have to waste time explaining the basics to you.

○ If you need a trademark, have you gone to *www.uspto.gov* and searched for your possible company and/or product names? Do you have a list of possible names that have cleared your initial search?

○ Do you have logos, drawings, or prototypes ready to show the lawyer?

○ Have you researched your competition, or what the closest invention is?

○ If you need a patent, have you searched the patent database on *www.uspto.gov* and *www.google.com/patents* and printed out results to show the lawyer?

It's important to set up the lines of protection in the early stages of business. With a little research under your belt, you will be able to fit more into that one precious hour of consultation. Follow through with the attorney's advice and protect yourself. You wouldn't send a child out on a bike without a helmet, so don't send your product into the marketplace without its protection. After all, it's your baby too!

Be wary of companies that promise to handle everything from patenting to product submission to bringing products to the marketplace. Some of these companies offer their services in late-night infomercials. Many have a checkered past, so check with your patent attorney and the Better Business Bureau before dealing with them. The Internet is littered with nightmarish stories of people who had bad experiences with invention-submission companies. Check out *www .IPWatchdog.com* for some interesting information.

Different Ways to Own a Business

Once you've got a handle on your intellectual property rights, you'll have to consider the ownership form of your business. Again, I suggest you contact a lawyer to discuss the options because I am not equipped to go into detail, but I will give you some basic information. (That can serve as my disclaimer once again!) The ways that you can own a company are the following:

- Sole proprietorship
- Partnership
- Limited partnership
- Limited liability company (LLC)
- Corporation (for-profit)
- Nonprofit corporation (not-for-profit)
- Cooperative

Though you won't need to finalize this decision until Step 6 (on your Resale License you will need to state the type of ownership that you have), let's look at your options now so you can weigh them. Don't panic; you can change this status later if you need to.

At first, it's simple: If you are going into business by yourself, you can be a "sole proprietor." If you have a partner or partners, you must look into the other options listed. According to the legal website *www.nolo.com,* the ownership categories are clearly defined as follows.

Sole Proprietorship

A sole proprietorship is a one-person business that is not registered with a state agency, whereas a limited liability company (LLC) or corporation has to be registered. You don't have to do anything special or file any papers to set up a sole proprietorship—you create one just by going into business for yourself. Legally, a sole proprietorship is inseparable from its owner—the business and the owner are one and the same. The owner of the business reports business income and losses on personal tax returns and is personally liable for any business-related obligations, such as debts or court judgments.

Sole proprietorships and partnerships make sense in a business where personal liability isn't a big worry—for example, a small service business in which you are unlikely to be sued and for which you won't be borrowing much money for inventory or other costs.

Partnership (Beware)

A partnership is simply a business owned by two or more people who haven't filed papers to become a corporation or a limited liability company (LLC). You don't have to file any paperwork to form a partnership. The arrangement begins as soon as you start a business with another person. As in a sole proprietorship, the partnership's owners pay taxes on their shares of the business income on their personal tax returns and they are each personally liable for the entire amount of any business debts and claims.

If you choose this option, be sure you *completely* trust your potential partners. You are, quite literally, trusting your partner(s) with your business life. Partnerships are easy to form but can be nightmares to dissolve. Think hard about partnerships and define them clearly in writing. Consider who's doing what—both now and down the road.

If they can do it, So Can You!

Surprised and thrilled by the emotional reaction his cakes brought to people, attorney Warren Brown realized he had something special. He began moonlighting from his law practice (litigating health-care fraud on behalf of the federal government) and started baking cakes from scratch. In 2000, when he could no longer juggle both commitments, he took the leap and gave up law. Warren Brown is now the host of *Sugar Rush* on the Food Network, and he also owns Cakelove and Love Café in Washington, D.C.

Limited Partnership

Limited partnerships are costly and complicated to set up and run, and are not recommended for the average small business owner. Limited partnerships are usually created by one person or company (the general partner), who will solicit investments from others (the limited partners).

The general partner controls the limited partnership's day-to-day operations and is personally liable for business debts (unless the general partner is a corporation or an LLC). Limited partners have minimal control over daily business decisions or operations and, in return, they are generally not personally liable for business debts or claims. Your business attorney can handle the paperwork and explain the intricacies of various options.

Corporations and LLCs

Forming and operating an LLC or a corporation is still more complicated and costly than the sole proprietorship or partnership, but worth the trouble for some small businesses. The main benefit of an LLC or a corporation is that these structures limit the owners' personal liability for business debts and court judgments against the business.

What sets the corporation apart from all other types of businesses is that a corporation is an independent legal and tax entity, separate from the people who own, control, and manage it. Because of this separate status, the owners of a corporation don't use their personal tax returns to pay tax on corporate profits—the corporation itself pays these taxes. Owners pay personal income tax only on money they draw from the corporation in the form of salaries, bonuses, and the like.

Like corporations, LLCs provide limited personal liability for business debts and claims. But when it comes to taxes, LLCs are more like partnerships: The owners of an LLC pay taxes on their shares of the business income on their personal tax returns. Corporations and LLCs make sense for business owners who either:

1. Run a risk of being sued by customers or of piling up a lot of business debts, or
2. Have substantial personal assets they want to protect from business creditors.

Nonprofit Corporation

A nonprofit corporation is a corporation formed to carry out a charitable, educational, religious, literary, or scientific purpose. A nonprofit can raise much-needed funds by soliciting public and private grant money and donations from individuals and companies. The federal and state governments do not generally tax nonprofit corporations on money they take in that is related to their nonprofit purpose, because of the benefits they contribute to society.

Cooperative

Some people dream of forming a business of true equals—an organization owned and operated democratically by its members. These grassroots business organizers often refer to their businesses as a "group," "collective," or "co-op," but these are often informal rather than legal labels. Most states have specific laws dealing with the setup of cooperatives, and in some states, you can file paperwork with the secretary of state's office to have your cooperative formally recognized. Check with your secretary of state's office for more information.

Are You Really Ready for a Partner?

Since the question of partnership is common among start-up entrepreneurs, I'm going to discuss it further. When it comes to business ownership, emotional issues are as important as the legal issues. Many people immediately assume they will need a partner, either to finance or to help get their company off the ground. But before you take on a partner, however, think long and hard about what that means for your business.

Partnership Survey

Get together with your potential partner and ask each other the following questions. Each of you should answer honestly and then discuss the differences that may come up. *Hint:* This should be a fun activity!

1. Is this idea your top priority?

---

2. Are you planning to work nights and weekends? How many hours per week will you devote to the company?

---

3. What is your goal for this company?

---

4. Which of us is more capable of dealing with the financial issues? Marketing? Dealing with people?

---

5. How will we solve an issue if we disagree? Who will have the final say? Who could we go to for trusted advice if we cannot agree on something?

----

6. List your top three strengths that you will bring to the table.

----

7. List your weaknesses or areas where you feel you will need support.

----

8. List the qualities you most admire in me.

----

9. What qualities about me scare or intimidate you?

Working with someone has pros and cons. Of course, it is nice to have support and add a different perspective, but you will need to compromise on some or many issues. Begin some dialogue, break the ice, and move forward with a true understanding of the way your partnership will operate.

Be sure that the person you're partnering with is really on the same page as you are in regard to financial issues, marketing goals, work style, and anything else of importance to your business and product. Many friendships have ended after partnerships were formed because these things weren't hashed out beforehand.

Give thoughtful consideration before becoming a partner, especially with someone who may have different goals and ethics. Talk freely and openly about how to handle hypothetical situations. Ask the tough questions before becoming partners. Complete the Biz Brainstorm on page 69 with your partner; then discuss your differences and how you will work together on your ultimate goal of business success.

Nondisclosure Agreements

You might be thinking, "I have a great idea, but I don't want to deal with the hassle of bringing it to market. I'll just sell it to a big company." I have heard this many times over the years and it is usually a real long shot. The biggest hurdle is simply getting a company to listen to your idea in a confidential setting. Big companies have their own large R&D (research and development) departments, so they are usually not interested in hearing from the general public about a product idea, especially if it is not patented.

That is when you would want to use a nondisclosure agreement. Here's the lowdown on several different scenarios.

With Unpatented Ideas

If you *do* find that a company is willing to hear about your unpatented idea, first have them sign a nondisclosure agreement (NDA). An NDA is an agreement stating that you are showing another party something confidential only for the purpose of a possible future relationship and that they are not to make use of the information for other purposes. NDAs are used in a wide variety of circumstances where two unrelated parties are discussing private information in order to see if they want to enter into a business relationship.

Companies are very reluctant to sign these agreements because they may be working on a similar idea and do not want to be accused of stealing the idea from you. Each company's protocol is different when it comes to dealing with "outsiders."

With Patented Ideas

You are in a much better position to get a company to talk with you if you have a patented product that may be helpful to a large corporation. If your idea is covered by your patent, an NDA wouldn't be necessary.

Other Uses

There are other uses for NDAs that are closer to home, namely, the people helping you build your business. Your employees and independent contractors should sign some form of an NDA or confidentiality agreement since they will be coming into contact with your confidential and proprietary information. In fact, it is not uncommon for entrepreneurs to insist that friends and family sign an NDA as well. While having friends and/or family members sign a formal agreement may seem over-the-top paranoid, it is an effective way to communicate the need for secrecy. After all, if your idea is easily compromised by a simple slip of the tongue, you certainly wouldn't want your mother using your idea as the subject of small talk with friends, who could then inadvertently pass your idea on to others.

I know this information isn't necessarily the "fun" part of following your dream, but it's necessary. The important thing is not to get overwhelmed with the legal aspects of intellectual property and business ownership. Do lots of research on your own and do your best to learn about these legal issues, and then hire a professional to get a qualified opinion and to execute your filings. This will be money and time well spent.

STEP 5

manufacture your idea into a product

I have not failed, I have found 10,000 ways that don't work.

—THOMAS EDISON

When people tell you how they brought a product to the marketplace, no one seems to discuss in detail how they actually got it manufactured. Everybody has a unique way of finding their manufacturing sources; often their journey takes one step forward, two steps back, over and over, until the issue is figured out. To find a great manufacturer, you'll need to do research, test materials, make phone calls, and be resourceful. There is no one formula for finding a manufacturer—you will have to find your own way through that maze based on your particular needs. But I'm here to say you *will* be able to do it and it will be a rewarding learning experience.

Goals as You Enter the Manufacturing Phase

Before we go on, let's outline our goals for this step in the process.

1. Figure out how to make your product.
2. Learn and understand exactly which materials are best suited for your product and why.
3. Make a prototype and test it.

4. Find a company that can produce small runs initially, at a fair price, in an appropriate time frame (and is also capable of offering discounts for larger quantities in the future).
5. Familiarize yourself with governmental regulations.
6. Figure out your product's packaging.

List the Physical Components of Your Product

It is helpful to look at the individual components of your product. For example the list for my gloves would look like this:

Components of Moisture Jamzz Moisture Gloves

- Fabric
- Glove pattern
- Fabric cutting
- Fabric sewing
- Inner care label
- Packaging

We'll spend more time on elements of this list in this chapter—for example, fabric—so you'll want to know what you need.

If they can do it, *So Can You!*

Leon Leonwood (L. L.) Bean was an outdoorsman looking for a better-quality hunting boot in 1911. He made a pair for himself and he knew others would appreciate the boot, so he advertised it in a mailer for outdoor hikers. He sold 100 pairs of his new boots, guaranteeing their quality. Unfortunately, the shoe's bottom separated from the shoe and ninety of those 100 pairs were returned. Bean knew he had a great idea with these special shoes, but he needed to perfect the manufacturing. He made the necessary improvements and continued to sell the shoes as well as other outdoor products. Instead of fizzling out at the first sign of a problem, Bean forged ahead and built a reputation for quality products and excellent customer service.

Make Your First Sample

You have described your idea in writing, sketched it, discussed it, and thought long and hard about it—now you need to make it. With your first sample (and this really depends on your specific product), try to make it yourself to the best of your ability. It doesn't need to be perfect, just good enough for you to get a sense of how it will look. This may involve hand-cutting some materials and rough-looking finishes, but that's okay—you just want to see how it looks as it comes to life. This sample will help you figure out which materials you need, how much of each material, and how they will be bound together. With this information, you can begin searching for manufacturers who can provide what you need.

million-dollar TIP Every industry has associations you can use as resources for networking, referrals, and information on issues that affect your industry. These associations usually represent and promote the interests of their specific group. Some associations may be local for a specific region only and some associations are formed with a national presence and may or may not have local chapters.

Some big associations that may help as a starting point depending on your product are:

- Consumer Electronics Association: *www.ce.org*
- Craft and Hobby Association: *www.hobby.org*
- Game Manufacturers Association: *www.gama.org*
- International Housewares Association: *www.housewares.org*
- International Music Products Association: *www.namm.org*
- International Spa Association: *www.experienceispa.com*
- National Association for the Specialty Food Trade: *www.specialtyfood.com*
- National Confectioners Association: *www.candyusa.com*

- National Specialty Gift Association (gift basket industry): *www.nsgaonline.com*
- Sporting Goods Manufacturers Association: *www.sgma.com*
- Toy Industry Association: *www.toyassociation.org*
- Travel Goods Association: *www.travel-goods.org*

Finding Manufacturers

You'll need to use several research methods to find your manufacturer. How much time you spend with each method will depend on what you need, how much time you have, and where you live. A well-balanced research job will likely yield the most productive results.

Referrals

The best way to find a reliable manufacturing source may be by a referral from a colleague, another manufacturer, or a trade organization or association. A referral usually implies a sense of responsibility and it puts the contractors on notice that you will be reporting back to that referral about your satisfaction with their performance. Look for manufacturers' advertisements in trade magazines. While an ad doesn't necessarily mean the publication is endorsing that company's work, it may at least be a starting point. First try to get a referral from a source whose work you appreciate and whose opinion you trust.

The Internet

The Internet is the easiest and fastest resource for finding materials and manufacturing. The good news: You'll find a huge number of manufacturers. The bad news: You'll find a huge number of manufacturers. How do you tell the good from the bad, the reputable from the fly-by-night companies? It's not always easy.

Trade Associations

Search for associations affiliated with your product category. Go to their website(s) and learn about what resources each one provides. Keep a database for reference when you need advice for networking, referrals, or regulations that govern the industry.

Touch base with one or two organizations via phone and see how they can help you learn about your new industry and become affiliated with it. Sometimes a call to an association is better than an e-mail; the staff is usually friendly and happy to help. Sign up for newsletters and read blogs so you will be abreast of happenings within your industry.

The Thomas Register

Begin by searching in the manufacturing industry's bible, the *Thomas Register*. This trusted series of books, now available online, is like the encyclopedia of manufacturing companies in the United States. It has been around for more than 100 years and should be your first step as you research domestic manufacturing.

Visit *www.thomasnet.com* and begin searching for what you need based on your rough sample. What if you don't know what materials you need? Just use the categories (such as automotive, electronics, hardware, chemicals, metals, plastics, rubber, and *many* more) shown on the homepage—narrowing immediately that way will make the task much easier. After navigating the site for just fifteen minutes or so, you will have a better idea of where to begin calling.

(A note: Although the *Thomas Register* lists U.S. companies, I have found that some companies do the majority of their production overseas. Clarify the location of the company's main manufacturing facility if that will make a difference to your product.)

Other Online Companies

What if you find a company online that is not listed in the *Thomas Register*? You can research its reputation by asking the company for references and checking out the company's listing with the Better Business Bureau, available at *www.bbb.org*. You can review how many customers filed complaints and whether the dispute was resolved.

Research on Foot

You can find manufacturing companies online, but if possible, I recommend you visit the plant, meet the plant manager, and begin to develop a relationship. There is something to be said for physically observing all aspects of manufacturing and having a face-to-face meeting with the person who could be responsible for bringing your product to life. In addition, business is cyclical—you may not always be doing a lot of production, so you probably want someone who can be flexible with your cycles of production.

Once you have found a few contractors that may work for you, ask to meet them at their factory. The factory should be clean and offer good working conditions and decent pay. You don't want any part of working with a factory that has unlawful work practices. If the company wants to be paid in cash, it's a big red flag.

Safe and Healthy Working Conditions

Whether you're able to visit your manufacturer or not, you must determine whether it provides safe working conditions for its employees. This process is somewhat easier if your plant is in the United States but can be very difficult for overseas plants.

The U.S. Department of Labor handles the enforcement of laws regarding the safety and health of workers in America. The division called Occupational Safety and Health Administration (OSHA, *www.osha.gov*) regulates private industry's safety and health conditions. Here are some things to watch for when visiting a U.S. manufacturing plant:

- OSHA rules and regulations should be posted in the factory for workers to see.
- The work environment should be clean.
- Workers appear to be wearing appropriate safety gear.
- Machines appear to be functioning properly.

If you cannot visit, get some printed material, like a sample invoice, company letterhead, and the owner's business card, then become a private investigator. Perform your due diligence as best you can by researching the company. Check them out through the Better Business Bureau. There is no law that businesses have to be accredited by the BBB, but if they are, it means that they have made a commitment to act in good faith to resolve consumer complaints.

The BBB does not evaluate nor endorse member businesses, but a clean record on their site is generally a good sign.

Though you are certainly not an OSHA inspector, use your common sense and gut instincts to gauge whether things appear to be running smoothly. You, of course, do not want anyone working on your product under unfair conditions, not to mention that it can be a public relations nightmare to be involved with a factory that abuses the rights of its workers (remember Kathie Lee Gifford's clothing line disaster?).

Questions to Ask Manufacturers

Once you've narrowed your search to one or two factories, be ready to ask the manager some questions, either in person or on a prearranged phone call. You are looking for a manager who is organized and willing to communicate with you about your needs and how the plant operates. Be ready with as much information about your product's materials as you have. Here are useful questions to ask:

- Can you produce some samples for me? (A small sample run, maybe six pieces to use for selling purposes.)
- What is the cost of the samples? (Expect that the cost will be much more than if you were having them produced in a large quantity.)
- How long would it take you to produce an initial, smaller run of, say, 500 pieces? 1,000 pieces?
- Would you be able to handle an order for 10,000 pieces? (You want to be sure that they will be able to handle larger orders with a quick turnaround time as your business grows. Let them know you are just starting and that your business won't be regular at the beginning, but once you get orders, you expect volume to increase. How will they fit your production into their current workload?)
- Inquire about their working conditions. Are the workers compensated according to law in the form of payment and hours worked?

Manufacturing Contacts

Fill in this chart (or customize it for your needs) as you investigate manufacturing companies:

Company name	
Contact and phone #	
Pricing	
Quantity per week	
Suggested material	
Specifications (weight, finish)	
Manufacturing location	
Lead time	
Materials they recommend (reasoning, explanations)	

This dialog will offer a lot of information about whether you can work with this company. You may not get every answer during that first conversation, which is fine—their follow-up response time will also be telling. Did it take them a few days to get you an answer or a few weeks? Was the answer ready when they told you it would be?

The representative you are talking with will likely be your contact person, so you need to be comfortable with her and feel she is responsible and reliable. Your reputation depends on theirs: If they miss production deadlines, you have no product to sell or ship, and a retailer will not want to work with you. You may only get one chance to work with a retailer, and you don't want that opportunity wasted because of an inefficient factory.

Domestic vs. Overseas Production

If you were able to find a local or domestic factory to get you started with your samples or a small run, that's great! But, it's no secret that with today's economic globalization, much of today's manufacturing is done overseas. Turn over any object and you will likely see "Made in China." The cost of labor abroad is usually much lower than in the United States, but there are other issues to think about too.

Resources for Overseas Manufacturing

Here is a starting point for finding overseas manufacturing:

- *www.made-in-china.com*:
  Online trade platform for Chinese manufacturers.
- *www.china-strategies.com*:
  U.S./Chinese strategy and operations consulting firm.
- *www.madeinmexicoinc.com*:
  A full-service company based in San Diego, California, that specializes in Mexican manufacturing.
- *www.hktdc.com*:
  Connects buyers and suppliers throughout Asia.

Manufacturing issues are complex and every entrepreneur's situation is different. Research the options just as you would for an American company and make an educated decision. Then continue to monitor and have alternative plans should things not work out.

Pros of Domestic Manufacturing

Whenever possible, I highly recommend staying in the United States with your manufacturing. First, to support our economy, and second, for a more hands-on role in your manufacturing. You can also meet deadlines easier (because you do not have to build in shipping time) and can deal with manufacturing headaches (such as issues with quality control) more efficiently.

Unless you are willing to be a frequent overseas traveler, you will not know if there are children working in the manufacturing plant or the number of hours or conditions that workers must endure.

million-dollar **TIP**

It seems that once a month, we hear about the recall of another product made in China. Whether it's the lead found in kids' toys or the melamine poison in both dog food and milk, none of it is good, neither for the victims nor for the companies whose reputations have been damaged. (Just think of how much liability insurance you'd need to deal with the 54,000 people sickened by that tainted milk!) Both the United States and China have recognized the need for more oversight and regulations, but the change will not happen overnight. If you use overseas manufacturing, make it your top priority to be sure your product meets all necessary American regulations.

Pros of Manufacturing Overseas

Clearly, price is the most obvious benefit of using an overseas manufacturer. Because labor costs are so much less in many other countries, they can offer you a very competitive price. Also, many factories produce such a huge volume of products that they may be able to group the purchase of your product's materials with other companies' materials to give you better discounts. The tables will give you a quick look at some of the other pros and cons.

MANUFACTURING IN UNITED STATES	
PROS	CONS
Faster lead time (no oceanic shipping delays)	Higher labor cost
More accessible for supervision and visits	
Mandatory working standards	
You can say "Made in USA" on product	
Easier to make changes/correct problems with manufacturing	
No language barrier	

MANUFACTURING OVERSEAS OR IN MEXICO	
PROS	CONS
Lower labor costs, bigger profit margins	Longer lead times (magnified for trend/style industries)
	Different standards and regulations
	U.S. Customs needs time to review imports and can hold your goods for variety of reasons
	Lack of control, possible lack of knowledge of day-to-day operations
	Cost of shipping impacted by oil crises
	Lower level of respect for intellectual property rights, which puts your IP in jeopardy, spurring knockoffs

I'm clearly a proponent of manufacturing in the United States, but I recognize that the domestic production cost can be a deal breaker. Gather the facts and make an educated decision.

Materials List for Your Product

Dissect your product and list all the possible materials it needs. And I mean *really* dissect it—down to the inner label or the screws. Don't leave out a detail. When you break down the product into all of its parts, it's much easier to know what you need for the final product. Research those materials, just as you did for manufacturers (online, through trade associations or magazines, by foot, and so on).

Be sure to research the components of competitive products, as well. For example, check out what other baby bottles are made of if your idea is a new version of a baby bottle.

Learning about Your Product's Materials

You probably have a good idea of what materials you'll need to create your product based on the list you made in the Biz Brainstorm: Materials List for Your Product. Learn as much as you can about those materials—the more familiar you are with your product, the better you will be able to sell it.

Keep an Open Mind

Don't assume that you know the exact material you should be using, even if you think your materials list is "final." Be open-minded as you do research just in case you find something better or more effective. Test samples and ask a lot of questions. Again, face-to-face meetings are the most beneficial.

While you do need to know your product inside and out, you may not be an expert on every single component of your product, and that's okay. Ask the real experts to educate you to the degree you need to be able to sell it. You just need to understand:

- Why you picked the final materials for your product. (For instance: Are they lightweight? Cost-effective? Durable? etc.)
- How to explain the benefits of those materials to your customers. Those benefits become even clearer when you have tried the wrong version of something.
- The availability of the material, and trends in its pricing (as those factors will affect your product's production and pricing).

Feel the different materials to experience why you like one over another. If you have found a few options that would work, ask the expert to explain why he would choose one material over another. Take copious notes, because a small detail can easily slip between the cracks early on, but once you understand more, you will grasp why that little detail is meaningful.

How to Choose the Right Materials for the Final Product

Your initial round of research calls about the pros and cons of different materials can be very enlightening. You can make just about anything these days, so don't be deterred without a full investigation.

Also, keep in mind that slight variations in materials can make a big difference to a final, finished product. Try to make your product in various materials and see the differences yourself.

Once you've done your homework, it's time to make some exciting decisions. And remember, though you may be committing to these materials for a certain production run, you could change them later if you learn something different about your product. Right now, it's important to move ahead.

As you discuss pricing with manufacturers, ask for quantity discounts, so as you grow you will have pricing incentives built in. Pricing usually lowers considerably once you reach quantities of 2,500, 5,000, and 10,000, so ask for prices at those quantities early on. Expect to pay higher prices initially and for small runs.

Making the Prototype

Once you find the materials that consensus has shown are the best for your product, make a more accurate prototype than your initial made-at-home sample.

Who Will Make It?

In a best-case scenario, you have been able to make final prototypes yourself (for example, if you're making candles in your kitchen). If your rough samples are good enough, you've saved yourself a step. But keep in mind that you need the prototypes to accurately reflect the final product, so be sure you've used final ingredients or materials.

If you can't make it yourself, your materials supplier or manufacturer may be able to make it for you. If not, go back to *www.thomasnet. com* and use the keyword "prototype makers." You'll see a list of companies that specialize in making prototypes and who will do small runs. The companies also list the materials that they work with.

You could also ask your patent attorney for recommendations—since most products that need a prototype need a patent, she may have some ideas. Most prototype companies will charge per piece that they produce.

Testing Your Prototype

At this point, you've got a real, working sample of your idea. Take a moment to reflect on how far you've come from that idea bouncing around in your head. You still have a long way to go in your journey, but you've reached an important milestone.

As you test the prototype, take a "devil's advocate" stance by:

- Treating it in a "not so gentle" way to see if it will hold up.
- Showing it to friends and family to get opinions.
- Thinking about possible problems and how to prevent them by making it the absolute best it can be now. (Think about L. L. Bean and his original shoes.) It's easier to make changes in the beginning. Don't be in a rush at this stage.
- Taking it into a small, local store that could conceivably carry your product and getting the owner's opinion.

Dealing with Difficulties

Finding a manufacturer that meets your needs in all respects is not easy. Even after you find your manufacturing partner, you may still encounter frustration. Know this going in, and you will be mentally prepared to solve the problem.

Here's where the problems often arise: The goal of a manufacturer and the goal of the entrepreneur are not always the same. The manufacturer wants to produce as many pieces of goods as possible in a short amount of time (most manufacturers get paid per piece). The entrepreneur, on the other hand, wants each piece to be perfect and wants to receive the products in a reasonable amount of time and at a good and fair price.

Come to Terms

Agreeing on price, time frames, and quality control requires a lot of negotiating and give-and-take. It is a frustrating process, but it can be a win-win situation for both parties. Compromise where you can, and stand your ground where you can't. Quality is never negotiable.

If you really want to work with a specific manufacturer—you know that they have a great reputation and track record—you won't have a lot of bargaining power until you have provided them with a quantity of work and income. At that point, you will have gained some leverage to renegotiate price or time frames.

Don't Give Up

If you're running into obstacles, quality problems, or scheduling difficulties, commit to fixing the problems. I ran into plenty of problems as I began making prototypes of my gloves. Manufacturing was by far the most difficult and frustrating phase for me, as it is for many entrepreneurs. Be patient, yet persistent. This process is essential to getting your product out there.

Compare Manufacturers' Prices

Use the exact material specifications (size, quantity, weights, finishes) to compare pricing options from several manufacturers. Get three quotes if possible. If you get the exact same options on each proposal, you will be able to compare pricing and see if one company's pricing is higher or lower than the others'.

If there is a big discrepancy between proposals, find out why. It usually means that you were not comparing all elements of the manufacturing; that some specification has been left out.

Don't make the final decision based on price alone. Price is obviously important, but it's not everything, although at this point in time it feels like it is, I know! Trust me; receiving quality product on time from a manufacturer is worth more than saving a little money.

If they can do it, *So Can you!*

Gert Boyle's parents fled from Germany in 1937 and landed in Portland, Oregon, where they began Columbia Hat Company. They soon began manufacturing products on their own and expanded into outerwear. Boyle got married in 1948 and her husband took over the company as it grew. In 1970, he died of a sudden heart attack, leaving her with three children and a business that was heavily in debt. She stepped up to the plate and, with no business experience, worked hard to revive the business to support her children. In 2006, Columbia Sportswear's sales topped $1 billion.

Price Point

Now that you know how much it will cost to manufacture your product, you can begin to finalize the pricing. You probably already have an idea of where your product's price point will be from researching your product's marketplace and seeing the competition.

As you determine a wholesale cost (what you will charge stores for your product), it is important to know your competitors' price points and the retail pricing (what the consumer pays) of similar items. We are all in business to make money, so you don't want your great product to fail because the pricing is off. Better to make a small margin on larger quantities than try for a huge margin and sell only a few. Your pricing will depend on your costs and your margin.

How to Calculate Cost

One general way to calculate your wholesale price is to add up the following three things:

1. Cost of materials per unit (such as fabric, labels, thread)
2. Cost of production per unit (such as cutting the fabric, labor/sewing contractor)

   (The cost of both materials and production will give you your breakeven point.)

3. Profit margin (The amount of money that you need to make on top of covering expenses. This number will also need to cover a portion of your fixed business costs such as phone, office supplies, and so on.)

Let's say the wholesale price point will be $6.25. Stores will mark that up at least 100 percent and retail it for upward of $12.50. (Don't forget, you will charge separately for shipping and handling to customers. The "handling" part can help to cover your cost of boxes, tape, labor.)

Price Tactics

Once you've got your "magic number," you could initially try selling at a higher wholesale price than the formula gives you, to see if the buyers will purchase at the higher price. They know their market, and will tell you if you're off.

If you need to have a tighter margin (#3 on the list), try to get the buyer to order in larger quantities, saving you money on production (remember the high quantity you produce, the better per-piece price you will get from the manufacturer).

If you're getting stuck, try working backward. For example, say your product needs to be in the marketplace, retailing at $50. You can then figure you will be "wholesaling" it to retailers for around $25 (because they will mark it up at least 100 percent). Deduct your costs (mentioned above) from the $25 and see your profit margin. Decide if that works for you.

Overcome Obstacles

There isn't one formula that will work for all businesses. If you find that your wholesale cost is too high and you aren't able to compete in your marketplace, you will need to reduce your production costs, and/or other business expenses such as materials so you realize a better margin. It's a give-and-take process.

When I initially sold Moisture Gloves, the price was considered high for the product category, so we had to defend the pricing. But we quickly found the "tipping point"—when people understood our niche, they got it. The buyers knew consumers would be willing to pay more for a quality product with fun prints. So don't be afraid to go into new territory with pricing—just be prepared to justify the price point. You can then see what the market will bear.

Quality Assurance

Now that you've got a product, you need to ensure that it's up to your standards at all times, from the first to the last. That means you'll need to act as your very own Quality Assurance department. In the beginning, you'll likely do this job alone, because no one else will be as picky about the product, no one else will know the nuances of the product, and maybe no one else is employed by the company.

Quality assurance, or quality control, means checking each product before it is shipped and making sure it is not defective in any way. Quality control begins with the first prototype. This step is so important because your reputation is on the line. If you say your product is well made, it better be!

Although the job is tedious, it is critical. Yes, you may have to check out thousands of pieces, but instead be proud that you are selling that many. No one wants to have product returned, and negative word of mouth is not good for business. If your manufacturing company gives you some defective products, you have a few options. First, you could ask them to repair it. If that's not possible, you should receive a credit for all defective pieces (unfortunately you will have to absorb the loss of the actual materials).

Never send out anything that has any sort of material defect or even a typographical or alignment error on a tag. If a buyer or account sees that you don't care about the little things, they may think you are sloppy with big, important details as well. So run a tight ship and send out only quality goods.

Inventory Management

Inventory balancing is an ongoing challenge that plagues even large, well-established companies (you've heard of things being "out of stock," right?). When you receive an order, you want to be able to fill it, yet you don't want to have your garage full of inventory that just sits there getting old and dusty. There is a fine line in balancing supply and demand. But once you have regular accounts, it is important to stock up on your inventory and to keep track of it.

How to Use Software

You can buy software programs for managing inventory (of course initially I made my own "custom" charts). If you start out selling only one style of one product, your inventory system is simple accounting. You will initially produce say 1,000 units and will probably not be reordering until you have sold many of those units. (You will know the lead time your factory needs and try to plan accordingly.)

Things get more complicated when you are selling many different versions or designs or sizes of your product. Like many small businesses, if you use QuickBooks software for accounting, invoicing, and packing slips, you can add on the QuickBooks inventory program, called Fishbowl Inventory. It is popular with small- to medium-sized businesses and versatile enough to suit many industries. You may need very precise and constant inventory control if you are dealing with food, perishables, or products that have a short shelf life or a product with fragrance that fades after a period of time, for example.

Keeping it "close to the vest" with inventory (supply and demand) issues, will really help your cash flow. In today's economy, it is more acceptable to simply fess up and tell the buyer that you don't have excess inventory on hand, but you will go into production right away and the order will ship in two to four weeks. This is where that great relationship with your manufacturer comes in. They need to be able to immediately go into production. Two to four weeks is a common lead time right now, as it is understood that small businesses can't afford to stock excess inventory.

million-dollar TIP

Even if it seems early in the process, consider investing in the software. Many small businesses use QuickBooks software for invoices, packing slips, accounts receivable, and internal reports. When you need inventory software, Quicken Fishbowl Software is a good choice. You don't want to get caught short, and miss orders and deadlines because you didn't know how much stock you had.

Starting Out

When you're just starting out, sell from prototypes or samples whenever possible. However, if your product is inexpensive, like my gloves were, produce a small run so that you can give samples to buyers and let them try it out. If your product is expensive to manufacture, you can exhibit at a trade show (more on that in Step 10) and make sales from the sample/prototype.

If you need to wait for orders to produce any significant quantity of your order, be up front with your buyers about how long it will take for them to receive the product. Most companies are okay with waiting four weeks for delivery, especially if they know ahead of time. You should have all of your manufacturing "ready to go" so when you get your initial orders, you can go right into production and fill the orders in a timely fashion. By "ready to go," I mean having *all* proofs/samples approved and all the kinks worked out so that when you receive the order, you can give the buyer an accurate ship date and you can tell your manufacturer to "Go into production!" without further ado.

Storage

Put any extra money back into production so you can have more product on hand. With luck, you can find room in your garage or den for inventory as you continue to find buyers. If your product is large or requires temperature control (e.g., candles or lip balms that could melt if you store them in your garage during summertime), you may have to rent a storage unit and, if necessary, a temperature-controlled unit.

Government Rules and Regulations

You will also need to research any governmental requirements and guidelines that your product needs to follow. For example, with our product, there are rules and regulations governing the garment industry that we needed to implement. Most garments need to have an inner label that states fabric content and care instructions. There are rules and regulations for food production as well. If you have a new kind of granola, you can only bake it at home for so long—soon you have to go to a professional kitchen. You would also need to look into requirements with the FDA (U.S. Food and Drug Administration), available at *www.fda.gov*. Even cosmetics have to check in with the FDA for labeling and ingredient requirements.

Find the Rules

The most comprehensive site for these rules and regulations is on the Federal Trade Commissions website: *www.ftc.gov*. Within that website, on their "Quick Finder" link, click "Rules." Next, on the left margin, click on "FTC Rules" and read the Electronic Code of Federal Regulations. This document offers a long list of many different industries and their regulations. Check out trade association websites for an insider's look at what you need.

Besides the FTC, here are a few more helpful governmental organizations to know about:

- U.S. Small Business Administration (*www.sba.gov*): Assists and protects the interests of small businesses.
- Better Business Bureau (*www.bbb.org*): A member organization that hopes to advance marketplace trust by offering reports and information to consumers about businesses.
- U.S. Food and Drug Administration (*www.fda.gov*): Responsible for the safety regulations of many items including but not limited to food and drugs.
- U.S. Consumer Products Safety Commission (*www.cpsc.gov*): Protects the consumer from unreasonable risks from products within their jurisdiction.

Take It Seriously

This is not an area where you can cut corners. Learn what government regulations and requirements affect your product and its industry, and meet all criteria in your prototype. If some rules don't need to be implemented early on, plan for them later so you're prepared.

Packaging Ideas for Your Product

Search for similar products and see how they are packaged. You may want to buy a few competing products to look closely at the different options. You need to see what's out there and drill down from there. You can also check *www.thomasnet.com* and search for packaging companies (they have more than 5,000 listed). If you know what kind of package you want, narrow the search with keywords like "plastic box" or "paper box" or "recycled packaging."

Maintain a database for packaging companies just like you did for manufacturers and materials suppliers. Your needs may change later and if so, you will have the information on hand.

Packaging

Once you have the product manufactured, you'll likely need to pack it in something to sell it. Not all products will require *complete* packaging, however. For example, if you have a new line of jewelry, the pieces might be shown on a display rack and sold to customers in gift boxes. Items such as backpacks or clothing will not be totally enclosed in packaging, but you will have some sort of company label or hang tag.

There are a few important considerations for your product's packaging:

- Know your product's demographic. Your packaging should appeal to that segment of the marketplace.
- Express your product's message. (You will discuss this with your graphic artist when she helps create your logo and branding. More to come on this in Step 8.)
- Only use what you need. People are also concerned with being "green" and helping the environment; nobody wants to see excessive packaging that is just going to be thrown away.
- Think about how your product will be displayed in stores.

Package Considerations

Ask yourself the following questions to get an idea of the packaging you need.

1. Will your product be displayed in bins or standing upright on shelves?
2. Might the product be on hooks and therefore need a hang tab? (Hang tabs can be purchased separately for versatility of packaging or built into the actual packaging.)
3. Will the product need to show through the packaging so customers can see what's inside?
4. Does the packaging need to be made with eco-friendly products?

You should also go into relevant stores and see what type of display fixtures they use. Notice if everything stands upright on the shelves, or in small boxes or bins, or on peg hooks. If you want to sell to Williams Sonoma or Bed, Bath & Beyond, for example, you need to tailor your packaging accordingly. It needs to be functional, yet fit in with the store's overall look and theme.

Make a Decision

Do your research from the Biz Brainstorm: Packaging Ideas, and make several packaging mockups before finalizing your decision. The more packaging companies you speak with, the better idea you will have about how to best package your product. Utilize their in-house art departments as much as possible. Ask for drawings or mockups—though you will most likely have to pay a fee, it's worth it to get a working sample. Graphic designers (more on them next) are usually pretty savvy about packaging materials as well and can be very helpful with suggestions. Have friends and family choose from a few options and have them explain why they preferred one over another.

Ultimately, your graphic artist and packaging company should work together with you to come to a decision based on your research and field testing. You want to be proud of the packaging and have it be able to be a true representative of the look and feel you want for your product, line, and brand. Packaging can always be revisited if you learn more information later. Do the best you can now while staying on budget and maintaining consistency of look and message.

Using a Graphic Artist

Graphic artists can run the gamut from someone who freelances from home to big full-service design firms. You'll likely need one to help you create your product or company's logos, branding theme, and/or packaging. As a bootstrapper, you'll probably have budget restrictions that eliminate the full-service option until your company has grown. Though you may have a good idea for a logo, consider using a professional to finalize it. As with any other expert, graphic designers are trained to know how best to present text and images so they are understandable, readable, and versatile. Plus, they may think of something even better than what you had in mind.

What You Should Look for in a Graphic Designer

As with any other professional, do your homework to find someone appropriate for your needs and budget. Look for these factors:

- **Good experience, good references, and a portfolio with designs that appeal to you.** Be sure to check the portfolio. Even if you're not an expert, you can evaluate whether the work is appealing, functional, and modern.
- **Good communication skills.** You will be talking with them frequently.
- **Honesty and creativity.** Your input is the most important, but they are the experts and can add something to a design that you may not have thought about. They should be open with their suggestions and you should welcome them.
- **The ability to handle rush jobs.** Occasionally you may have a big retailer that asks for a proposal or something that requires a quick turnaround. You want to work with someone that understands these important deadlines and is willing to get to work fast. (But be ready to pay a possible "rush fee"!)
- **Patience.** Designers can be very technical people and you are probably not familiar with the design jargon. Find someone who is willing to explain the lingo and the specifications of a job to the degree you want.
- **An interest in your work.** The person does not need to want to buy your product, but does he seem to share some excitement with you? If so, it will likely be reflected in his work.

Where Do I Find a Graphic Designer?

Unexpectedly, I found a graphic artist because I fell in love with the package design of a product located close to my booth at a trade show. In mentioning this to the owner of the small company, I ended up meeting her graphic artist on the last day of the show. She worked out of New York, but the distance wasn't an issue. If you see something you like, don't hesitate to try to find out who created it. Here are some other tips:

- If you live near a college or university that offers a graphic design program and you have a relatively simple job, ask a professor to recommend a student in his last year of the program. He will likely be eager for the job and also relatively inexpensive.
- Ask friends who work at larger companies that have a design or creative department for referrals. Sometimes the company designer is willing to do freelance work on the side to earn extra income.
- Ask for referrals locally from friends, family, colleagues, or local businesses.

If none of the above options work, you can search online or in your local phone book for resources. Be sure you review the person's portfolio online or in person to get a sense of her experience level and quality of work.

How an Arrangement with a Graphic Designer Will Work

Your agreement with the designer could take many different forms depending on how extensive your needs are, the person's business arrangement (is he on his own or does he work for a firm?), and how involved you want to be. Here are some things you can expect:

- If you work with a freelance artist, she may work from home and control her own workload.

- She can work on a flat fee per project or an hourly wage. Fees will vary depending on her experience and location.

  - *Flat fee:* If your job is on the bigger side and requires a lot of time—such as designing new packaging, which may take many back and forth tweaks before you love it—you are better off negotiating a flat fee. That way, the price will include all the design discussions and trials. Also, designing a company logo takes time and a lot of trial and error, so use a flat fee for that as well. Have your designer write detailed proposals for the flat fee projects so you know exactly what is included. Discuss the amount of times you will be able to tweak, change, and revise things—there will be a limit.
  - *Hourly rate:* An hourly rate is appropriate for smaller jobs that will take anywhere from less than one hour to up to three hours. For example, creating a promotional flier or setting up company letterhead would be best done at an hourly rate. Once your business is more established (and if you are not savvy with graphics programs), you may find yourself frequently in touch with your graphic designer for quick jobs that may take only ten to twenty minutes. Ask if you can be billed for less than an hour for these small things. My graphic designer (whom I love dearly!) lets me run a tab and then bills me monthly.

- The designer may offer many services—logo creation, marketing materials, web design—or only one or two. Try to negotiate package deals for multipart requests rather than "a la carte"—you'll end up saving money.

Again, arrangements vary widely. Be sure yours is fair, meets your deadlines, and leaves you excited about seeing your brand in words and pictures.

Logo Ideas

Write down descriptive words for your graphic designer that connote the feeling you want to evoke. Make note of other logos that you like. Write down colors that you feel are appropriate for your logo based on the industry and target audience.

Creating Your Brand

Now that you have a handle on your packaging and have found a designer, you can pull together both parts to form your brand. To do this, consider your product's message. Your packaging and logo needs to reflect this "message."

For example, if your product is an upscale, sophisticated new kitchen utensil, the packaging needs to promote that same feeling. If you have a baby product, you will want your packaging to look soft and reassuring, and have a "sweet" feeling to it (through the use of specific colors and fonts). If you are trying to appeal to athletic teenaged boys, you will need a strong, bold message.

To give your designer some direction, check out how certain colors and fonts make you feel. You will begin to notice similar fonts used on juvenile products and you can spot scripty fonts on packaging trying to convey some sort of formality. (More on this in Step 8.) After you have figured out your demographic and your message, discuss these goals with your graphic artist. They'll be a great starting point for him. You can even list certain words you'd associate with your product. Examples of great descriptive words are: whimsical, upscale, feminine, fun, sophisticated, premium, pure, organic, high-end, clean, crisp, bright, masculine, bargain, retro, and edgy.

UPCs

I'll mention UPCs (Universal Product Codes) while we're talking about packaging, because you need to be sure you leave space somewhere on your label, tags, or packaging for it. UPCs are the distinctive barcodes you see on virtually every product. They can be scanned by cash registers. They are uniquely numbered so that each company has its own seven-digit identification number and then each product the company sells has other digits added to the seven for a unique product code.

Fees to register for your company's unique UPC number range from $150 to $1,500, depending on the number of items you plan to sell and the company's gross sales numbers. Check out these websites for information on obtaining a UPC:

www.upccode.net
www.buyabarcode.com
www.gslus.org

million-dollar **TIP** Keep notepads in your car, on your nightstand, and in your kitchen, or anywhere you spend time. You will have little ideas popping up in your head at odd times, and the notepads will ensure you don't forget any. Keep a flashlight or pen with a light handy on your nightstand—I bet you will have some 3 A.M. ideas like I did! Transfer the good ideas into your workbook or computer, so everything stays in one place.

Once you've dealt with the manufacturing, you can breathe a deep sigh of relief. That is usually the most difficult and trying phase of your journey. Many people become so frustrated at this point that they end their journey. Congratulate yourself and celebrate!

At this point, you will know:

- That your product can and will be made.
- Why you are using the specific materials you chose.
- What your prototype and packaging looks like.

You will continue to use and test everything until you feel it is perfected, but for now, you're up and running. You are now ready to officially make yourself a CEO and get your "office" set up.

STEP
6

create your executive office

The only place success comes before work is in the dictionary.

—VINCE LOMBARDI

In this chapter, I'll set out my checklist for you to follow to bring your new business to life as a functioning entity. After you've completed the checklist, you'll look like a real company to the outside world and feel like you have the structure to begin your business success.

Setting Up Your Home Office

Unless you have the money to rent some office space, your home will have to do the trick. You may be setting up your "office" in your bedroom or a corner of your family room, den, or kitchen. Wherever it is, it *is* an office. You're a CEO now, after all! It is a place of business and must be treated as such.

It may feel silly at first, but keep in mind that no one needs to know that your company is extremely small and that you are working from home. If you follow the instructions in this chapter, you will have what I call a "perfectly professional façade." With Internet, voice mail, and cell phones, you can magically appear to be a "real" business with relatively little effort.

What You Need

Arrange a clean area, fresh from clutter with good lighting and the supplies you need. Put in the time up front to organize everything—it will pay off later. Here's a basic list of what you'll need; tailor it to your specific situation.

- A separate business computer from your family's (you don't want to compete with your kids and spouse for time on it), with reliable and high speed Internet and business e-mail access.
- A printer—the "all-in-one" style is useful, as it can scan, copy, and fax as well.
- A phone with a separate phone number. This is an added expense, but it's important (more on separate lines later in this chapter).
- Office supplies you'll use. Don't run out to the office store and spend $500 on cool-looking Post-it Notes if you'll never need any.
- A calendar, either on your computer or a paper one.

Benefits of a Home Office

Working at home and saving the cost of rent always makes sense whenever possible. You can also be really productive with a home office, because you can go back and forth between household tasks and office work quickly. You also save time and money by not commuting, and you can be available for your kids as well.

Challenges of a Home Office

Of course, working at home also has its drawbacks. Even in your "office," you may be disturbed by the noise of kids playing or the TV. You may also feel like you *have* to work while at home. When you leave your office to enjoy dinner with your family, consider it the same as leaving a totally separate office and driving home. Try to carve out "working hours" so you establish those boundaries. It takes some time to master the balance, and will require the cooperation of everyone in your home, but before long, you'll be comfortable.

The "Doing Business As" (DBA) Application

You need to file two main documents as soon as possible: the DBA application and the resale certificate/seller's permit. These forms enable you to be considered a real business and sell goods.

The first is the DBA application, which allows you to legally use your company name. DBA stands for "Doing Business As" and is also referred to as a "fictitious business name." A DBA allows you to have a name for your business other than your own name without formally setting up a corporation or business entity.

For example, if I wanted to sell flowers under the name of "The Fabulous Florist," I would file a DBA. The DBA registration allows me to use that name and open a bank account with that now-legal business name. Unlike trademarks, a DBA name is not rejected if it is similar to another one in your area, but you still need to be diligent that you are not taking someone else's name.

Each state's laws differ regarding DBA requirements, so find your state's laws and be sure you follow them. In California, for example, once you file the DBA, you have to publish it in a newspaper for a few weeks to announce it.

You can find many online services that will handle DBA filing and publishing for a small fee. One to try is *www.legalzoom.com.*

Resale Certificate/Seller's Permit

After you fill out your DBA form, you can obtain your resale certificate, or seller's permit, which will allow you to buy supplies at the wholesale cost directly from manufacturers under your new business name. Since the resale certificate needs to be issued in your company's name, you must do the DBA form first. Both retailers (stores that consumers buy products from) and wholesalers (the companies that sell their products to the retailers) must obtain resale licenses (also known as seller's permits). This permit allows both retailers and wholesalers to purchase goods with room for profit margin or at what is known as the "wholesale price." You need a seller's permit even if you are selling something only for a short period of time like a holiday season. On this form, you will be required to state the type of ownership that you have for the business. So, if you have a partnership, you will need to decide which specific type of partnership you will be forming before you fill this form out.

Seller's permits are issued by each state's Board of Equalization, Sales Tax Commission, or Franchise Tax Board. It is illegal to sell products without a seller's permit in any state. Go online to find out which government office in your state handles these forms.

There can be a small application fee charged for seller's permits. Go to your favorite search engine and put in the keywords "resale license" or "seller's permit" and your state. For example, if you need to purchase organza giftbags to put your jewelry in when you sell them to stores, you will buy the bags at wholesale cost. You will go directly to the manufacturer, let them know you have a resale number, and purchase the bags. The price will allow you to mark it up and sell it to the retailer, who then marks it up again for the consumer. When you buy wholesale, you usually will have to buy "the minimum required for wholesale pricing." Every company decides their minimum amount required, as will you for your buyers.

As with DBA filings, you can find services that will handle it for you for a small fee if you are really pressed for time and you have some cash to spare.

Renting a Mailbox

Using a mailbox service or a P.O. box rather than your home address for your business address is a smart idea for several reasons:

- You want your business mail separate from your personal mail.
- They are inexpensive.
- You never want to use your home address for privacy and/or security reasons.

The caveat with P.O. boxes? Try to use the street address where you are renting the P.O. box rather than simply "P.O. box ###."

There are many privately owned storefronts like Parcel Plus companies that allow you to use "their street address" and put your "mailbox number" as just #. That way it looks like a suite number, and you do NOT have to say P.O. BOX #. That screams, "I don't work in a real office," and you'd rather emphasize the professionalism of your business. Today, many P.O. boxes have "real" street addresses and you just need to put the box number as, say, #100, so it looks like a suite number!

Stay away from:

My Company, P.O. Box 501, Any City, USA, 00000

Get something like:

My Company, 100 Main Street #501, Any City, USA, 00000

It's especially useful if you get a P.O. box on a street known for commercial business, not a residential-sounding street, such as court or terrace. It sounds like I'm making a big fuss over a small detail, but these small items can make a significant difference in how your company is perceived.

million-dollar **TIP**

If a buyer is in town and wants to see your office, which rarely happens, don't worry. Just say, "I work out of my home, let's meet at. . . ." But until then, mum's the word.

In addition to the U.S. Postal Service (*www.usps.com*), other companies such as the UPS Store (*www.theupsstore.com*) and Mail Boxes Etc. (*www.mbe.com*) offer this service.

Be sure to get a box that is close to your home, because you will want to keep up-to-date on your mail and you don't want to waste time commuting to it frequently. Usually, if you are waiting for a specific package (or a check!) you can call the office to ask if you have any mail. Most mail-service places will also accept your UPS and FedEx deliveries, which is handy. If you order from a company that will not deliver to P.O. boxes, you usually scoot around that rule by having your mail-service box. Another nice feature of a mail-service box is that you don't have to pay extra for home-office deliveries because the mail service signs for it.

Once you have your DBA, seller's permit, and postal box, you are ready to proceed.

Accepting Credit Cards

Now that you have a legal company name, set up a business checking account so that you can be issued company checks and possibly a company credit card and the capability to accept payment by credit cards. Banks require you to open what's known as a "Merchant Account" to do so. Once you set this up, when you charge a customer on your credit card machine, all credit card payments will go directly into your business bank account.

Setting Up a Merchant Account

To set up an account, talk to the bank where you have your business account, or feel free to use another if they have a plan more suited to your needs. You don't have to have a business account with, say, Wells Fargo, to use them as your merchant account bank. The second bank can wire the credit card funds to your business account, wherever that may be.

Generally speaking, a merchant account is an arrangement where a bank facilitates credit card payments from customers to the merchant's bank account. When a customer pays by credit card, they will see your company name and charge amount on their monthly statement. You cannot use your merchant account for accepting payment for anything other than your specific business transactions.

There are four basic types of noninterchangeable merchant accounts dealing with the basic categories of transactions:

1. Retail (brick-and-mortar storefront)
2. Internet (from a website)
3. Wireless (just like a retail account but the terminal works off cell phone activity if your business is a traveling business or in a kiosk that doesn't have phone service)
4. Mail order (catalogs)

Brick-and-mortar businesses that have a retail merchant account for their in-store credit card terminals must establish a separate Internet merchant account to accept payments via credit cards online.

Internet merchant accounts can only be used for Internet transactions and usually have a higher transaction fee than retail merchant accounts. Once established, your Internet merchant account will be linked with your website's shopping cart program to process payments using encrypted data and the funds are deposited into your bank account. (More on this in Step 7.)

Call a few banks and ask them to e-mail or fax over their schedule of rates and charges. Spend some time comparing these schedules since set-up fees, transaction fees, and other rates and charges can differ greatly from bank to bank. Most banks are very motivated to get your online business, because they want the reoccurring transaction and monthly maintenance fees they will make off your Internet sales. Use this very rare position of power over the banks to play the banks off each other to get the very best deal.

Hint: Many of the banks will waive the set-up charge if you simply ask. See how far you can get the banks to lower their fees and charges.

Processing Payment

To physically process payment, you'll need a transaction platform. These come in various shapes and sizes—you've seen them all over the place at stores' cash registers. They have a place to swipe a card, a keypad, and a viewing screen. Using the machine is simple, and it comes with detailed instructions when you receive it. You can also take phone orders as well—you do not need the actual card to charge the account number. You can just enter the number manually along with the expiration date, billing zip code, and sometimes the additional security code on the back of the credit card.

Accepting Payment Online

Your merchant account may also handle online transactions if you've got a website up and running. Someone who specializes in e-commerce (buying and selling on the Internet), or perhaps even your website designer, can set that up on your website. We will be covering this in more detail in Step 7.

Choosing a Shipping Carrier

Now that you have a product to sell, you'll need to choose a regular shipping company to use. Open an account with the USPS, UPS, FedEx, DHL, or another reputable shipping company. At first, you will most likely be sending out more press kits than orders, but it is professional looking to have the printed labels that you can now make online with these companies. You can easily track the delivery status online as well.

The Major Carriers

UPS (*www.ups.com*) and FedEx (*www.fedex.com*) are the major players in the shipping world. UPS provides the software (called "WorldShip") you need to print your own shipping labels, or you can create shipments online from their website. Until you need daily pickup, it may be more economical to set up your account on their website rather than use the software. The shipping rates are higher, but you don't pay a monthly fee as you do to use the software. Soon, you will likely work your way up to "deserving" the software, printer (for a small weekly charge they will rent you a special label printer), and better shipping rates.

FedEx offers similar options—you can use their FedEx Ship Manager online, or use their FedEx Ship Manager software program. Visit their website and fill in the "Find a FedEx solution" questionnaire. FedEx will recommend a program based on the needs you enter (how many packages you'll ship per day, whether it's domestic or international, how much it weighs, etc.).

Get to know your local UPS or FedEx sales representative. They can help you with the details and pricing options. After you develop a shipping history as your business grows, you can negotiate certain discounts with the carriers. A good relationship with your area representative will certainly help.

For a weekly or monthly fee, UPS and FedEx will stop at your door every business day and pick up your packages. These accounts usually enjoy reduced rates compared to "Occasional" accounts. If you don't have shipments going out every day, but are almost at that point, it's probably still a better option to go with the daily pickup. The better rates you get with the daily account will likely justify the weekly service charge. A billing representative from the shipping companies will be able to either look at your account history or evaluate your estimated shipping volume and help you decide. Expect to be charged higher rates if you live in a remote area.

The U.S. Postal Service

Another alternative to UPS and FedEx is the U.S. Postal Service website (at *www.usps.com*), where you can easily set up an account in a matter of minutes and be able to print shipping labels and postage from your own computer and printer. You can leave packages with those labels at the post office without standing in line.

This option is great for small packages that weigh less than a few pounds, where the rates are very competitive with UPS and FedEx. Also, the USPS is a great option if you have heavier items that can fit into a USPS "flat rate" box, where you are charged a flat rate for as much as you can stuff into that box. Your mail carrier can also pick up your packages if you schedule it ahead of time.

The current USPS package tracking system is not as sophisticated as that of UPS or FedEx because it will not tell you "in transit information," such as where it is at that particular moment; it will only confirm that the package is delivered. USPS has no weekly service fee for picking up packages.

Setting Up Your "Shipping Department"

You probably won't have a warehouse fully staffed with a "shipping department," so as with most other tasks early on, this one lands on your plate. Set up an area either within your "office" or near where your inventory is stored and designate it as your shipping department.

Once you begin your marketing efforts and product shipping, you'll be using this area frequently. You need your packages to look professional and arrive intact. Purchase supplies so shipping packages can be easy, fast, and accurate. Once you have your resale license, you will be able to purchase boxes and shipping supplies wholesale and in bulk. (You do not want to be paying retail prices for boxes and supplies. A good supplier to try is *www.uline.com.*) The best thing about Uline is that they deliver the next business day.

Here is a list of shipping supplies:

- Boxes and envelopes in the sizes that are appropriate for your shipments
- Clear shipping tape or customized reinforced tape with your company name
- Scissors

- Craft paper or stuffing material so the contents don't rattle around or break during transit
- Packing slip pouches (if necessary)

With these supplies, you won't have to dread sending packages; instead it will be an easy, efficient assembly line.

Lines of Communication

In today's business world, consumers expect that a company will have a toll-free number; perhaps a local number; voice mail to leave messages; a fax number; an e-mail address; and as much as possible, a live person to speak with if the need arises. Your company is no different. Here's what you'll need.

An Actual Phone

Buy a phone that's easy to use and has a "hold" button. To get this function, you may have to buy a two-line phone, even if you only have one phone line. Sometimes you will need to place the call on hold and get a document or quickly reference something, and it's more professional to put the caller on hold than drop the receiver on your desk and have the caller hear you fumbling around. You may also want a hands-free device so you can speak without trying to balance the phone between your ear and shoulder. Try to get a phone with caller identification capabilities or you can get the separate caller ID piece from your phone company. It is nice to know whose call you missed if they decide not to leave a voice-mail message.

You could start with a cell phone (using a separate number than your personal cell phone) until you are ready to add a line to your home. I do recommend the landlines eventually, however, because they get better reception and feel more professional. A landline says you are attached to the ground somewhere with an actual office.

A Dedicated Phone Line

Set up a designated phone line for the business under the business name. Try to get a number that ends in "000" or "00" if possible—these seem more "commercial" than residential. When you are getting the new number, ask the phone company representative to search for available numbers with those criteria. If your company name has a number in it, try to work the phone number around those particular digits to make it easy for customers to remember.

A Toll-Free Number

When you order something from a big business, they always have a toll-free number so the consumer doesn't pay for the call to buy or even inquire about the product. Consumers expect to see an 800 number (or now, sometimes 866 or 877 and other varieties) when they call to order something. You don't want your customers to have any reason not to order your product, so give them a free call.

The business division of your phone carrier will provide you with a toll-free number. It is linked to your local number, but you never have to give your local number out to consumers, just the toll-free number. As with the local number, try to get a toll-free number that is easy for your customers to remember. It's a great advertising tool, too. For example, 1-800-MET-LIFE.

Give a few minutes of thought about what words you may want to get for your toll-free number. There is a nominal monthly fee, and you do have to pay for the calls from your customers.

A Fax Number

If you don't want to add another phone line to your home for a separate fax machine, you can fax electronically. You pay a company a monthly fee for a certain number, and beyond that you will have to pay per fax. You are issued a local phone number for people to use as your fax number. The company eFax (*www.efax.com*) is one to try.

Instead of the fax appearing on your fax machine (which you do not have), it is routed to your computer via e-mail or the hosting company's website, where you then can log in and print it out. People sending the fax don't know it is not going through to a fax machine.

If you fax electronically, you also need a scanner (which you may have on an all-in-one printer), because you may have only a hard copy of a document you need to fax. (If you have a document electronically, you needn't scan it to fax it.)

Even if faxing seems outdated, many retail outlets will fax purchase orders, so you need the capability. Oh, and never do the "same phone line as fax line" thing. It sometimes doesn't switch on properly and it screams "home office" when you give someone the phone number and say it's the fax number too.

Phone Etiquette

As long as we are talking about phones, let me give you a few tips about phone etiquette.

- Answer the phone with a standard, friendly greeting.
- Always return business calls within twenty-four hours. If you delay, you are sending the message that their call is not important and also that you are disorganized.
- When you answer the phone, you shouldn't have children's voices yelling in the background. Better for a call to go into voice mail than for a potential buyer to hear the chaos of the family home in the background as they are trying to do business with what they thought was a "real company." Your customers expect the same level of professionalism from all vendors, even if they are working out of a home office. Oh, and no doorbells, barking dogs, lawnmowers, and typical residential noises either. Be well insulated. Make calls from a closet if necessary. (Been there, done that!)

Voice Mail

Voice mail is an absolute necessity and if you have another full-time job at the moment, you'll need to check it once or twice during the day and do your best to return phone calls within a day. Special answering services can be very helpful; they make it look as if you have a receptionist and all sorts of extensions and departments (for example, "press 1 for placing orders; press 2 for our billing department," and so on: you can set these up so all options go to the same phone).

A cardinal rule for home office CEOs is to never say the word "home" while on your business calls. Whenever possible, have a live person answer the business line from 9 to 5 in your time zone. This may mean call forwarding if you are on the road a lot or working in other locations. If a buyer gets voice mail during regular business hours, it's not a great sign, but there are worse faux pas. If you cannot be by the phone physically, be sure to check your voice mail frequently so you can return missed calls promptly.

A Business Website

You will need a website sooner rather than later in today's high-tech commercial marketplace. Everyone wants to visit a website when they hear about a new product. Websites run the spectrum from basic versions that simply give contact information such as company name, company story, mailing address, e-mail address or e-mail link, and fax number to elaborate e-commerce sites such as Neiman Marcus or Target that sell a lot of goods online.

Start small and build your website as your company grows. At first, it is very important to secure the domain name (*www.domain name.com*) as soon as possible.

You want to be sure you can get your new company name as the domain name or something very close to it. For example if you are a retail store named Mary's, and the website *www.marys.com* is already taken, try to get *www.shopatmarys.com* or *www.marysof phoenix.com*; you get the idea.

Even if your homepage says "coming soon" or "under construction" for a while, just get it set up and have the company's contact information shown. We'll get into more detail about setting up your website in Step 7.

Business E-Mail

Set up an e-mail address that is "businesslike." Don't ever use your personal e-mail address, especially cute and personal ones, like martini26@searchengine.com. Once you have your company's domain name, which is usually your company name, your web designer can set up appropriate e-mail addresses using the company name in place of the standard server name, for example, Julie@ AcmePrinting.com. You need to own the domain name to use it in your e-mail address.

If you cannot set up even a basic website yet, use an appropriate name (like your full name) with a common server name (such as AOL, Yahoo!, or Gmail).

You're probably thinking: another e-mail address to check? Yes, you do need a separate one for your business. But just like "call forwarding" on phones, you can forward your e-mail addresses into one central inbox so you just have to open one account to check all your e-mails. The one critical issue with this consolidation is that you must go back to your business e-mail account to reply; otherwise it will show that you sent it from your other e-mail address and you'll confuse the sender.

Once your business e-mail is set up, read about your program's customization options. You will probably use two of these options regularly: the "out of office reply" and the "signature," which appears at the bottom of e-mails. If you are going to be out of town without access to e-mail (or don't want to be bothered with e-mail while on a vacation) or if you won't be able to check e-mail for more than twenty-four hours for some reason, set up your customized "Out of Office Reply." With this feature, senders are automatically sent an e-mail letting them know when you will be back in the office to return their e-mail inquiry.

You should also set up a standard "signature" that includes your full name, company name, website address, street address, phone number, and fax number that will appear at the bottom of each e-mail that you send out. Set it up once and it will automatically appear in each outgoing message that you send. It makes your e-mail like letterhead and makes your contact information handy at all times.

If they can do it, *So Can You!*

EBay.com began as a simple website that Pierre Omidyar set up at home for his girlfriend so she could connect with other collectors that shared her interest in Pez candy dispensers. He had a computer programming background and wrote the code for the auction website in just one weekend. It quickly became a popular destination for people to sell or buy just about anything. Today, millions of products are bought and sold daily on eBay. By 2006, eBay had earned more than $5 billion in revenue.

Business Cards and Letterhead

Even if you use e-mail frequently, you'll still need hard-copy letterhead and business cards on hand. They should include the standard information: company name, logo, address, phone and fax numbers, website, and e-mail address. You could also include your company slogan or tagline.

For business cards, simply use your name, without a title. Since you would need to list many positions, it is better to not list any. I liked the anonymity that you have without a title, especially when I was dealing with a buyer or a manufacturer. They didn't need to know that I had the final say on things as an owner would. When I needed to negotiate something, I could say, "I need to ask my production manager" or "our sales manager." They don't need to know that you are the CEO, because if you are the CEO of a decent-sized business, you will not be the one making sales calls or calling as accounts payable to collect a late payment from a customer.

Your graphic artist can design the layout and the artwork for the business card and incorporate the same colors and fonts on your letterhead and mailing envelopes. Keep the look of your brand consistent throughout all marketing materials (more on this in Step 7).

Your graphic artist can usually recommend a paper stock and e-mail the files directly to a printer. It costs approximately $200 to $300 for 1,000 copies of nice quality letterhead. The best pricing on letterhead is usually at 1,000 sheets because it costs only a bit more than if you buy 500. This will give you incentive to buy the 1,000 sheets and send out lots of letters and press kits! Use it up.

In conversations with colleagues and clients, use the word "our" instead of "my," as in "I will check with our shipping manager" or "Our company policy is. . . ." It makes it sound like there is someone in the "office" besides just you.

Stickers

You may also want to have your graphic designer configure some stickers as well. Stickers are handy for the front of press kits (discussed in Step 7) and for the outside of envelopes or boxes. If you don't need huge quantities, the designer can usually just lay out the

Chart Your Progress

Once you've completed most or all the tasks in this chapter, you will be well on your way to looking and feeling like a "real" company. You will be able to work with pride and confidence and no one will know that you alone are the entire company and that you are working out of your bedroom or garage. This checklist will help you keep track of what you need to do and enjoy your progress.

TASK	PROGRESS
File DBA	
Resale license	
Mail service	
Checking account	
Merchant account(s)	
Shipping account(s)	

TASK	PROGRESS
Shipping department	
Dedicated phone line	
Toll-free number	
Fax number	
Voice mail	
Website	
E-mail	
Business cards	
Letterhead	

artwork within the specifications of label sheets (there are many different sizes) that you can buy at the office supply stores. You can then print them yourself. If you need large quantities, your printer can usually fill that order or recommend someone who can.

Your business will feel "real" once you bring home the new letterhead, business cards, and envelopes, and set them up in your home office. You can now be reached via phone, fax, and e-mail—you're just like the corporate giants now. You are ready to move forward and get the word out about your new product. You need to begin to market it like crazy.

learn marketing 101

Marketing is too important to be left to the marketing department.
—DAVID PACKARD, HEWLETT-PACKARD

The dictionary definition of "marketing" is "the total of activities involved in the transfer of goods from the producer or seller to the consumer or buyer, including advertising, shipping, storing, and selling." In other words, marketing is getting the consumer to know your product and your brand name. It is a task that never ends. As you read this chapter, you will become familiar with all the aspects that define marketing, from finding your niche in the marketplace to mailing out your press kit to buyers.

Now that you are in a positive and committed frame of mind, are familiar with the market for your product, know your competition, and your office is set up, you are ready to move into the marketing phase. Think about how to introduce your product to the customers who need it or will want it, and will welcome it into their lives.

Become Part of Your Industry

One good way to begin thinking about how to market your product is to immerse yourself in information about your industry. Since eventually you want to become a key player in it, do your homework now. Even if you are still working another job at the moment,

and even if your sales are small or nonexistent, get a foot in the door
of your new industry. Take small steps like these:

- **Find the most popular trade magazines and newsletters and
  subscribe to them.** Those articles will help you learn the lingo
  you may need for marketing materials. See who the "big names"
  are and what they bring to the industry.
- **Research the big companies.** Look into which trade shows they
  attend or sponsor. This will indicate the show's level of importance within the industry. There is more information about trade
  shows in Step 10, but they should be on your marketing radar.
- **Make a list of stores, catalogs, and online retailers you want
  to contact.** Get on their mailing and/or e-mail lists so that you
  are up-to-date with their industry news. We'll talk more about
  contacting them in Step 9.
- **Be aware of trends.** Look for new product lines, what items are
  on the clearance racks, and where companies are spending their
  advertising dollars. Focus your marketing campaign on your
  product's attributes and why a consumer should buy your product
  over another. You need a good handle on what else is out there.
- **Determine where your product fits in.** Get perspective so you
  can position your product most effectively.

It can't hurt to start becoming a part of the industry—your par-
ticipation will only help you as you market your new product. You
will be able to quote the industry's research and speak intelligently
to colleagues or the media, the buyers will appreciate your knowledge, and you won't feel like an outsider.

"Mass" Marketing

If you have a product that can appeal to "the masses," you're saying
that nearly every man, woman, and child can use and/or purchase
it. For example, a product like Kleenex has mass appeal. When you
have a runny nose, it doesn't matter if you're old or young, man or

woman, rich or poor, living in Kansas or Manhattan—you need to blow your nose, so you need Kleenex.

The nature of your product really determines which market you will focus on, niche or mainstream. If you have something that will appeal to the masses, you will probably target the big chain-store accounts. If your item has a much smaller target market, you will start with smaller stores and specialty chains. Even if your product has mass appeal, however, you'll likely need to market to one particular segment, or niche, at first. For that reason, I'll go into depth about niche marketing.

If they can do it, So Can you!

Ahead of his time, before anyone cared about organic, Horst Rechelbacher found his niche. In the late 1960s, Rechelbacher was a hairstylist and salon owner. He began to question the safety of the chemicals they used daily in the salon. He studied the Eastern philosophies of yoga, meditation, and Ayurveda (a 5,000-year-old system of natural healing), and went to India to pursue these interests. He then began to make plant-based hair- and skin-care products with the help of his mother, who was an herbalist. In 1978, Rechelbacher launched Aveda, a line of plant-based beauty products. Today, Aveda is also known for its environmentally friendly manufacturing processes as well as its products. It was an innovative leader in the organic beauty industry. Aveda was acquired by Estée Lauder for $300 million in 1997.

"Niche" Marketing

A niche is a special, smaller "piece" of the marketplace pie where your product will have specific appeal. Mainstream or mass marketing companies think of pleasing the majority of people out there;

niche marketing is almost the opposite. Niche marketing is what you will focus on if you have a specialty item that caters to a smaller market segment. Just because a product has a niche market doesn't necessarily mean your product doesn't have potential to reach a large audience or be very profitable; it just means that it may not appeal to a big chunk of the world.

For example, a high-quality cashmere bathrobe would be marketed to spas and higher-end boutique-type retail stores, not to Target. Its smaller niche market is women who love being pampered and have disposable income to splurge; probably women thirty-five to fifty-five, which is a pretty small target audience.

It's great to start with niche marketing and then expand when the item gets popular there. At that point, word spreads and you can move into mainstream merchandising with confidence and market share. You may have to adjust your pricing for the new market (which is easier to do when ordering in large quantities). Mass marketing spawns knockoffs quickly. Think of the faux cashmere bathrobes that would follow at a lower price point, made out of a synthetic imitation yarn that feels similar to cashmere.

Here are some examples of well-known products that have been successfully niche marketed. They focused on smaller segments of larger, very successful industries, like beverage, shoes, and food, and some of them have now moved into the mainstream mass market.

Red Bull Energy Drinks: Cool and Hip

Red Bull, one of the first energy drinks available in the United States, was given out to extreme athletes as well as young, hip celebrities to give the drink its trendy cachet. It's now available in several varieties at countless retail outlets.

Bear Naked Granola: Premium and Organic Granola

Two college-aged friends made this natural granola and gave away lots of it at Whole Foods stores so people could taste it. Giveaways are a very effective marketing tool, especially for food. People needed to taste the granola to realize it was worth it to pay a higher price for the premium-quality organic ingredients.

Jones Soda: Soda in Personalized Bottles

Initially, Jones was a distributor and then decided to make its own line of drinks. The soda bottles have labels that feature photos of actual customers who sent the images to the company. (Visit *www .jonessoda.com* to see them.) Fun and unique, their marketing strategy began with what the company called "alternative distribution strategy." They sold their sodas in unlikely places like tattoo parlors and skateboard stores. Then with their popularity growing, they were able to move into mainstream mass marketers like Starbucks and Target, even though it is still technically a niche product.

Communicating to Your "Niche" Market

Once you've determined your intended market, you can strategize how to reach it by showing that your product serves a purpose that no other currently fulfills.

If the market for your product is *truly* untapped, it is a perfect opportunity for you to become the industry leader of the niche market or market segment that will be interested in your product. Obviously, it's easier for a small entrepreneur to gain a large market share of a niche and become the "original," than try to compete with big-name conglomerates that dominate the mass market right off the bat.

A great example of niche marketing is Samuel Adams beer. They market to an upscale beer-loving market, a segment of the marketplace that cares about the "handcrafted" quality of beer, rather than the mass appeal of Budweiser. According to their website, Samuel Adams is the largest craft brewer, brewing more than 1 million barrels of Boston Beer products, yet it still accounts for less than 1 percent of the total U.S. beer market. Samuel Adams is now a publicly

Marketing Your Product

Jot down the answers to these questions in your notebook to develop a marketing strategy:

- How will your product be known within its industry?
- Is it an improvement to something similar? If so, are your differences enough to make a real statement?
- Whose needs are you serving?
- Are their needs being met in a better way? A faster way? A more efficient way? What exactly makes your product stand out?
- Who will your niche market be? Boil it down to a sentence or two. (It helps to imagine a single imaginary person who will love your product. Then write down all his or her attributes— age, sex, income level, spending habits, needs and wants, etc.)
- How will you create the need for the product, if the product is something new and unique? (Think Red Bull: They created the need for highly caffeinated drinks for the younger crowd. Before Red Bull, we weren't drinking energy drinks besides coffee.)

traded company on the New York Stock exchange, yet they only cater to a very small portion of American beer drinkers.

When your company positions itself like that, it takes on instant credibility and makes a name for itself before knockoffs come (and they will). Samuel Adams spawned a bunch of other "handcrafted" specialty beer companies and microbreweries. Knockoffs and competition don't have to be the end of your business; they will just make you have to work harder and smarter for the same market share that you have owned for a while.

People are willing to pay more for quality, convenience, and healthy things to name a few, so make your "benefits package" part of your marketing strategy. Making someone's life easier or better is a great selling point. People often like the feeling of buying something "special" for themselves. If you are going to celebrate something, you may want "special" Samuel Adams beer, as opposed to the mass-market brand that is cheap and has no cachet. People are willing to pay for something that makes them feel special.

If they can do it, *So Can You!*

Many entrepreneurs (including me) came up with their product ideas when they said to themselves, "I can't be the only one with this problem!" "I figured I wasn't the only one with a curvy body," says Shoshanna Gruss, creator of fashion line Shoshanna. She was curvier than most girls her age as a teenager and had a hard time finding stylish, age-appropriate clothing and swimsuits, so she started her own line and marketed it to other women with body types like hers. It is now a multimillion-dollar business. She proved there were many people out there like her and that her line of clothing is more "inclusive" of most body types.

Creating Your "Elevator Pitch"

Now that you know your ideal consumer and why he or she needs your product, craft an "elevator pitch." This is a common term in the marketing world and comes from an imaginary elevator ride with a buyer or customer and you only have the elevator ride—say ten to twenty seconds—to sell this customer your product. That scenario is actually very realistic—not the elevator ride, but the time frame you may have to sell someone your product.

The point is, you won't have half an hour to go on and on about your product. You need to be able to boil it down to a quick explanation. If you are lucky enough to get a buyer on the phone, trust me, the conversation will have to be fast. The buyer will not be interested if you don't have a well-honed, zippy elevator pitch so he or she can visualize your product and make a quick assessment. If your elevator pitch is good, the buyer will likely initiate further discussion or ask you to send your press kit and samples.

To create your pitch, write a few sentences that promote the benefits of your product. Then edit it down to a quick one or two lines or phrases. Mine became "Moisture Jamzz are the upgraded, modernized version of the classic white cotton glove beauty secret."

Here are a few examples of how some big-name companies quickly and concisely describe their brand or product:

- *True Religion jeans:* Fashion-forward premium denim company.
- *Crest toothpaste:* Healthy, beautiful smiles for life.
- *Burger King:* Have it your way.
- *Gillette:* The best a man can get.
- *Kellogg's Frosted Flakes:* They're g-r-r-r-eat!
- *Visa:* It's everywhere you want to be.

Of course, these companies have major marketing divisions and advertising agencies at their fingertips, but you can see that it's possible to explain your brand or product in just a sentence or two. Besides the elevator pitch, many products are associated with their tagline (a memorable phrase to emphasize a product's key benefit).

Elevator Pitch for Your Product

Writing down some options for your "elevator pitch" really helps refine the definition of your product. You will use this quick explanation more times than you can imagine, so you want it to be easy to say and clear and concise in its wording.

Your elevator pitch can be longer, of course, but your ideal situation would be for your product to have these types of short, effective sentences and taglines.

Start by writing the top five words that describe your product's function or purpose. Then, move on to five words that describe the benefits of the product. Next, try to make a few sentences using those words and continue to boil it down until you have a couple of sentences that clearly describe your product.

Creating Marketing Materials

Now that you have your elevator pitch, logo, contact information, and price point, you can build your marketing materials. In order to effectively market your product you will need to have these materials—in various formats—readily available to send or e-mail to buyers and journalists who are interested in your product. You need such items as brochures, photos, fliers, press releases, and press kits available in both physical and electronic form. You'll use these in your various marketing efforts, so they should be accurate, readable, and powerful.

Quality Photography

The cliché "a picture is worth a thousand words" is true when it comes to marketing. You want photos of your product to be so good that they help sell it.

Use a Professional

You can either hire a professional photographer or buy a great digital camera and try it yourself. But beware: Do-it-yourself photography may save you some money, but it won't help sell your product if it's shoddily done. Amateurs often struggle with poor lighting, incorrect perspective, and inconsistency—don't suffer with these to save a few hundred dollars.

To make photos look "finished" have them taken by a professional. As with other professionals, see if your friends or family know someone trained in photography. If not, seek out local photography clubs or community college courses and post a request on an online forum or office location to see if anyone is interested. You may find talented people who do not necessarily run a photography business. If none of those options work, search online or in your local phonebook.

Work with the Photographer

You will be using these images frequently and for different marketing mediums, so they need to look sharp and interesting. Have your photographer take as many pictures as possible during a shoot and use a variety of scenarios, poses, or groupings of products so that you have lots of options to show different outlets and people will not be seeing the exact same image in several different places. Give this some thought before you schedule a shoot, so you can be prepared. Bring a list of the shots you want to take and any necessary props, models, or backgrounds.

Express Your Brand Through Your Marketing Materials

Just as you did while designing your packaging with your graphic designer, give her descriptive words to help her understand how you want the marketing materials to look. She will then use fonts and designs that evoke those feelings or words. You can even search online for fonts you think might be appropriate and list the names for her.

Fonts are very important to marketing materials because they are able to evoke vastly different feelings. A word written in script has a more formal and feminine feeling, so if your product is fun and masculine, script is not a good choice. For example, look how different the same word "feels" when seen in completely different font styles:

Beautiful   *Beautiful*   *Beautiful*

Colors are also important and have their own properties of evoking a feeling. For example, red is known as being the color of power and passion. Yellow is associated with happiness and energy. Light pinks and pastel blues feel juvenile since they are typically used for baby products. Be sure to discuss color and font with your graphic designer when working on your marketing materials. Your font style, color, and graphics will become your brand. Keep them consistent on everything from packaging to price sheets.

What to Actually Make

As you've no doubt seen, there is an endless supply of products you can use to market your materials. The spectrum ranges from the traditional (trifold brochures, one-page fliers) to the useful (pens, calendars) to the fun (Frisbees, temporary tattoos). Your product, its market, and your budget should help you narrow it down to those options that will get you the most bang for your buck. Here are some of the traditional pieces you'll need.

Trifold Brochures

You've seen these thousands of times, either in your mailbox or in cardboard holders on counters at stores. They're usually an 8½" × 11" sheet of paper folded evenly into three sections the long way. They're useful because you get both sides to fill, so you have room to use several photos and a good amount of descriptive copy. Here is a sample layout to consider:

- Side 1, fold 1 (front): company name, logo, website, and photo
- Side 2, fold 1 (inside, left panel): your elevator pitch and a list of competitive advantages
- Side 2, fold 2 (inside, middle panel): photos and contact information

- Side 2, fold 3 (inside, right panel): list of other products you sell or available varieties or colors
- Side 1, fold 2 (back): two options—can be filled, or can be left almost blank (just your return address and phone number) for an address in case the piece is ever mailed
- Side 1, fold 3 (piece tucked inside): more photos and customer endorsements

This is one of many options. Start by making a list of everything you want to include—your pitch, your competitive advantages, your contact information, photos, and so on. Then fit the puzzle pieces together on a quick mockup you make yourself. You'll find you may need more or less text and can fix it accordingly. You want to get your message across but you don't want the reader turned off if he has to read tiny type or if it looks disorganized and cluttered.

Once you have a working sample, your graphic designer can create it electronically and polish it off using the same colors and fonts as the rest of your branding material. Your designer can e-mail or upload the high resolution files directly to your printer who is supplying your letterhead and business cards.

Marketing Mailers/Postcards

You should also consider making postcards, which are especially useful as a direct-mail piece to send to small retailers. You can fit a few key pieces of information on them and they are relatively inexpensive to print and mail. They come in various sizes, but 5" x 7" is probably the most common.

You can send out the postcards by themselves, or include them in your press kits as well. Postcards are useful at trade shows too, because they can serve as a color brochure with a pricelist on the back. They are less expensive than giving away press kits and easier for buyers to handle. Buyers receive so much information at shows that it is beneficial to hand them just one piece that has a picture of your product, some pricing information, and your contact information. If your local printer does not handle postcards, here are just a few of the many companies that print them:

- Modern Postcard: *www.modernpostcard.com*
- Postcard Mania: *www.postcardmania.com*
- My Postcard Printing: *www.mypostcardprinting.com*

Your graphic designer can help set up the postcard, then e-mail or upload it to the printer you choose. It is fast, easy, and effective.

Purchase mailing lists with names of businesses within a certain industry from companies like Dunn and Bradstreet (*www.dnb.com*) or USA Data (*www.usadata.com*).

Other Fun Items

Though it's entertaining to see all the wild things you can print your logo on (see *www.branders.com* for a slew of them), save them for a time when you have a bigger budget. Though these items are fun to hand out at trade shows, you need to focus first and foremost on putting the facts about your product in the right hands. Unless you feel that fun items will truly do that and you can justify the high cost, skip them for now.

Mailing lists can be expensive, so here's another option. Look in your industry's trade magazines. Some will list members of the trade association once a year in the magazine. Or—shhh, don't tell—check a competitor's website and see if they have a "Where to Buy" section, where they list all the stores that they sell to. Those lists are a great starting point.

Creating a Website

If putting together a website seems overwhelming and expensive, it doesn't have to be any of those things! You can hire someone to build your website at a very reasonable rate these days. Unless you have already set up websites for some reason, let an expert take care of this for you. You don't want your site to be going offline all the time, loaded with broken links, or difficult to use. Your website is an essential facet of your company's image and it needs to be great.

Baby Steps to Building Your Website

1. Talk with colleagues or friends who have built their own website. They will probably have been-there-done-that tips for you.
2. Note what you like about your favorite websites. Is it the look, the layout, the fonts, the user-friendly system, the easy checkout? Look for the web designer's credit—it's often listed at the bottom of the homepage. Consider contacting him to design your site.
3. Talk to at least three web designers, and get pricing and a detailed list of what your site will include. Just like with manufacturing, you need to be comparing apples with apples when you get pricing for building your website. Ask them if they implement e-commerce applications or if they work with someone who does. It's nice to have a team that can work together. Discuss their level of experience with search engine optimization (which will be discussed in Step 8).
4. Register your website domain, and set up your e-mail address with your own company or domain name as soon as possible if you haven't already.

After the initial website is up, your web designer should work on an hourly basis as needed for website updates, pricing changes, and so on. Work with someone you like and trust, and someone who will be available to make changes or website repairs in a timely fashion.

Find an Available Domain Name

If you have already trademarked your company name, you probably checked the availability of that domain name already. If that domain is already taken, find one that isn't that will work *with* your company name. For example, if your company is Hotel Hudson and *www.hotelhudson.com* is already taken, look for something like *www.stayathotelhudson.com*.

If you have not yet decided on your company name, you can work backward by searching for available domain names on a domain registry site and then checking to see if the name is available in the trademark database on *www.uspto.gov*. Once you have found the right name, buy it. This becomes your website address.

Register the Domain Name

Register the domain name yourself (as opposed to having it in the name of your web designer), so that you own it and can control it. Even if you plan to have someone else design and build your website, it is critical that you register and manage the domain name yourself. There are many websites where you can search and register domain names, such as *www.1and1.com*, *www.godaddy.com*, and *www.register.com*.

Domain names cost around $20 to register per year, and you need to renew them. You will likely buy the domain name for a year or two as you launch, but be sure that you keep a calendar reminding you to renew, or opt for the automatic renewal feature offered on most domain registration sites. As soon as things are taking off and you feel like you are in this for the long haul, I would renew for the longest amount of time possible, which may be ten years. Doing so puts renewal out of your mind and also affords you a considerable savings versus renewing annually. Some of these services will e-mail you to remind you of the renewal, but track it yourself as well.

Design the Site

Once you own the domain name, your web designer will make it "live" by hosting it on a server. Some web designers host as well as design—that kind of one-stop shopping is a great option for a novice. Your web designer will need the information you receive when you register the domain (which explains how they point your domain address to their server).

Web hosting costs vary depending on the type and complexity of the website. For a very basic website, the monthly fee can range from $10 to $30. If all you need is a "static" website with no shopping cart, hosting companies such as HostGator (*www.hostgator.com*) and Server Intellect (*www.serverintellect.com*) are two well-known companies that are on the less expensive side and customer friendly.

When you're thinking about your site design, discuss the following variables with your web designer:

- Your overall vision about how the website will look.
- How many pages you think you want on your website (e.g., a homepage, contact us page, about us page, products pages).
- Your goals (e.g., mainly selling product). What you want the visitor to do or receive from your website.
- Discuss your budget.
- Discuss time frame.
- Discuss e-commerce and search engine optimization (in Step 8).

The bottom line is that you want to have an interesting, easy-to-use, professional website that is user-friendly and represents your product and company well.

Add E-Commerce Capabilities

E-commerce refers to the act of selling product on your website. If you will be selling online, have your web designer build your site to accommodate e-commerce functions. E-commerce can be very beneficial to your bottom line. There is nothing like waking up in the morning and seeing an order from someone in Australia or Taiwan. You can make money while you are sleeping or on vacation! Even on a shoestring budget, you can still have a very decent-looking, user friendly, secure e-commerce website up and running sometimes within a week or two.

Not all web designers are familiar with setting up e-commerce software, however. I use the company Interms (*www.intermsllc.com*), which builds websites and can add e-commerce capabilities. It is reputable and offers great customer service, including a lot of explanation as the site is built. It's nice to have a full-service company available when problems arise. The staff knows the site inside and out, and they can handle little glitches quickly.

Site-Specific Shopping Carts

There are elaborate ways to set up electronic shopping carts if you are selling many products, or less complicated systems, like PayPal. If your website's main purpose is to sell lots of products and if you will be expanding your product line frequently, you will need a more customized shopping cart than what PayPal offers. Shopping cart systems take more time and money to customize than working with PayPal, but if your business warrants the shopping cart, get it. Talk with your web designer about your short- and long-term goals regarding e-commerce so that you will have the appropriate setup. As we discussed in Step 6, you'll need an Internet merchant account to handle online purchases.

PayPal

PayPal is a service that allows users to pay or be paid from online transactions without sharing financial information. It's a good option if the following are true:

- You are only selling a few products.
- You do not yet have a merchant account with your bank.
- You cannot afford a more extensive and secure shopping cart system.

One main difference between a personalized shopping cart and PayPal is that PayPal handles the financial transaction—you never see customers' credit card information. It goes directly through Pay-Pal's system. However, if a consumer doesn't have a PayPal account, he or she will need to set one up before purchasing through PayPal on your website. It's easy to set up, but requires the consumer to leave your website, go to *www.paypal.com,* set up an account, then go back to your website to purchase. The good news is that many people have established PayPal accounts.

million-dollar **TIP** If your product is available through brick-and-mortar retailers, but you also want to sell it on your website, too, never undersell your retail partners. If your product sells in stores for $50, keep your price at $50 or higher.

Payment "Gateway"

Your online store will also need what's called a payment "gateway." A payment gateway is the link between your website shopping cart, the credit card companies, and your Internet merchant account. The gateway is completely behind the scenes and uses encrypted information (SSL) to secure the transaction information. Authorize.net, VCS (Virtual Card Services), WorldPay, VeriSign, and PayPal are examples of payment gateways.

Be Sure to Be Secure

It is critical that your website is secure for e-commerce transactions or customers will not feel safe buying products from your site. Naturally, customers are worried that if a website is not "secure," their credit card information will be available to others on the Internet. Having a secure website means that your customers can purchase products confidently and trust that their information is safe with your company. Without security, your website may experience what is known as "abandonment." The visitor will leave the website without purchasing, and you may lose a customer.

In order to be secure, websites need Secure Sockets Layer (SSL) technology and certification. This technology allows for encryption of sensitive information during an online transaction. VeriSign (*www.verisign.com*) is one of the largest companies to offer this Internet infrastructure. According to their website, they protect over 1 million web servers with digital certificates. The certification can cost around $1,500 for a year and $2,700 for two years and then needs to be renewed. Authorize.Net (*www.authorize.net*) is another well-known company that issues SSL certification.

This service is costly, but without it, the savvy consumer will move on. It is one of those things that online buyers look for right away on a website.

You can tell that a website is secure if:

1. The URL starts with "https://" (http:// is not secure).
2. There is a yellow padlock icon on the right side of the address bar (in Internet Explorer).
3. The company that issued the SSL certificate has a shield or an icon featured on the website that can be clicked to verify the authenticity of the certificate.

Your web designer can handle this during the building of the site or even later if you decide to add e-commerce down the road.

DIY Website Options

If, after reading about all the facets your website should have, you still want to attempt to do it yourself, you can find lots of directions and services to help you. How extensive your site design and function can be depends on your interest level, your technical ability, how much time you have, and your budget.

Patty Civalleri of 1-Take MultiMedia (*www.1take.com*) says that entrepreneurial types sometimes favor DIY options because they like to be in control of most parts of their business. However, she gently warns that, "unless you are experienced in website design, the time that it takes to learn and experiment is time away from your core business interest. People can spend hundreds of hours learning about the complexities of websites and you need to be sure that you can afford to do this. Otherwise, pay an expert and use your time doing what you do best, building your business."

If you want to give DIY a try, here are some popular options of all different levels:

- *www.godaddy.com*: look into their "Website Tonight" option
- *www.freetemplatesonline.com*: has free templates
- *www.templemonster.com*: pay a little money for a more professional-looking website
- *www.wordpress.com*: set up a blog as your website
- *www.adobe.com*: buy the popular site-design program called Dreamweaver (but you will need knowledge of HTML)

million-dollar TIP

No matter how trustworthy your website designer is, insist on getting all log-in and security codes for your website as well as instruction for how to access the inner workings of your site. Keep this information in a safe place. Without the log-in codes, you may be unable to access your website if something happens to your designer or you have a parting of ways. Why? Even if you own the domain name, the actual website "sits" on a server that may be locked. It would be a headache to fix.

A final option is a Content Management System (CMS), such as *www.joomla.org,* or *www.oscommerce.com.* With CMS, someone experienced builds your website and then you are trained to manage it. These can be complex systems that can handle user-interactive events. With user-interaction (RSVP, clicking onto calendar systems, e-commerce), there usually is a lot of updating and website maintenance. If you want to be able to do those updates yourself instead of frequently relying on (and paying) someone else, CMS may be the perfect option.

Once you have targeted your market and figured out your "elevator pitch," you can reach out to your audience through many outlets. Your website will be a key part of your efforts, and you've now got a good handle on that. Now let's move on to using your materials strategically online and on paper to get you sales!

make the most of your marketing efforts

The Internet is becoming the town square for the global village of tomorrow.

—BILL GATES

Once you've found the "niche" segment upon which you'll focus your marketing efforts and actually created your marketing materials and website, it's time to implement your strategy. You will be marketing online by utilizing search engine optimization, blogging, implementing a viral marketing campaign, and gaining exposure through social network sites. Plus, you'll be marking on hard copy the old-fashioned way by sending out press kits. We'll talk about both in this chapter.

In today's high-tech world, consumers spend billions of dollars online. Your product needs to be there! Much of your online marketing efforts (with the exception of setting up your website) can be done with little or no monetary outlay so it is the best bang for your buck. Creating a fully functioning website is by far the most important and most time-consuming of these ventures. You will be directing traffic to your website and its store if you have one.

Search Engine Optimization (SEO)

Once your website is up and running, investigate an Internet function called search engine optimization (or SEO), which refers to your site's ability to get the most quantity and quality of traffic from the search engines. SEO's main component is the keywords that people enter to find information online. Optimizing your website to get the best results from search engines mainly involves the coding within the content of the website so that the search engines easily find keywords within your site.

For example, if someone goes to *www.google.com* and wants to find moisturizing gloves, she may type in the keywords "moisturizing gloves." As you've seen, Google will return countless options. The goal of SEO is to get your company to be at the top of the "free" results list (the "Sponsored Links" of a Google search are paid for). SEO optimization experts plant keywords throughout your site that the search engines will "crawl" and pick up, therefore raising your position on the free pages.

Your search engine ranking (where your website appears on search results) is a result of complicated and ever-changing systems developed by the search engines. Many companies can handle advanced search engine optimization (for a fee, of course). Some well-known companies are *www.bruceclay.com, www.seoinc.com,* and *www.seomoz.org.*

You don't need to master the inner workings of SEO. Just know that it is vital that your web building team understands SEO well so that they set up your website accordingly. It can make the difference between your site appearing on page 20 of the Google search results or page 1.

Blogging

A blog is a website set up like a journal with frequent entries or updates about a particular topic. Blogs are interactive—viewers can read the content and make a comment about what's been "blogged." Many blogs provide commentary or news on a particular subject; others function as personal online diaries.

Blog Search

Before setting up your own blog (if you are not a frequent blogger), check out what blogging is all about. When visiting and interacting with blogs, you will notice features or layouts that appeal to you or aspects you may not like. Take notes so you can communicate with your web designer, who should be able to set this up for you.

Have you looked at other blogs relating to your industry? Blogging plays a big part in today's grassroots marketing campaigns. When bloggers mention a product or service they liked on their blog, then everyone who reads that blog will get their recommendation.

One way to get started is to visit *www.blogsearch.google.com* or *www.blogcatalog.com*. You can read blogs based on their general categories or you can enter keywords such as "beauty products" and read blogs talking about popular beauty treatments and products. If you search on the keyword "entrepreneur," you will find all sorts of blogs about entrepreneurial life and the trials and tribulations of some bloggers as they follow their dreams.

Don't feel like an outsider: You can add your own comments right away and begin to blog. Blogs usually have a link that allows you to add a comment after each entry.

You can often sign up to receive e-mail updates from the blog host so you know when the blog has been updated. Beware, however—blogging can be addictive and very time-consuming.

How to Set Up a Blog

You can set up a blog very quickly, or ask your web designer to lay this groundwork, and you can begin writing regularly. Two popular options are *www.blogger.com* (if you don't own a domain name) and *www.wordpress.com* (if you own a domain). Both offer templates that make setup easy. The address is often something like *www.sandyabrams.blogspot.com*. You can upload pictures or videos right away and have a customized look in no time.

The "problem" with blogs is that if you don't update them regularly or answer posted questions and comments, readers will lose interest fast. You don't need to invest an hour a day—time yourself to spend fifteen minutes writing about a simple topic of conversation that pertains in some way to your product, its industry, or your life as you start this new venture. You can also give advice and tips or share stories and opinions. It is a casual arena to chat about common interests. If you can get your consumers interested in your blog, you'll have a captive audience to announce new products, get feedback on potential ideas, and learn more about why they like your company.

Viral Marketing Campaigns

Viral marketing refers to spreading the word about a product by word of mouth (or e-mail). Though it can be done by conventional methods of magazines and newspapers, it's more typically associated with Internet usage today. Online viral campaigns are used for the same purpose as conventional marketing campaigns: to increase brand awareness and sales. And it's easier, faster, and cheaper to spread the word online.

With the explosion of online social networks, viral marketing campaigns are priceless . . . and the exposure is free! If you want to advertise in a magazine, you'll pay big bucks that usually only the huge companies can afford. Try to spread some good gossip about your product, utilizing a high-tech yet simple and creative viral campaign. For example, you can create a video that is interesting, funny, unbelievable, shocking, emotional, meaningful, whatever—just make sure it shows your product being used! Then put it on your company's website or your company's page at *www.facebook. com*, *www.twitter.com*, *www.myspace.com*, or on *www.youtube.com*, and get it out into the viral marketing world. Send it to your e-mail list and ask them to pass it on to their lists; soon, if it is creative enough, people pass it on for its merits rather than because they know you.

E-mail Promotions

You've no doubt signed up for e-mail lists for your favorite companies or services and then received special discounts periodically. You can do this for your product as well.

Create a promotional e-mail introducing your website and products to as many family and friends as possible when you launch. Ask them to forward the e-mail to at least five or ten of their friends and family (and, if they feel comfortable, to copy you so you can add those names to your company's database). As an incentive, you can offer a promotional code for a 10 to 20 percent discount if they buy something off your site. You need to be sure that your e-commerce system is set up to handle such a promotion—usually buyers are asked to enter a special code, which will activate the savings. If it is not set up properly for that, offer another savings option. The simple act of asking people to refer your company to their friends and associates can have profitable results.

Word-of-Mouth Success Stories

Nothing beats the marketing success of good, old-fashioned, positive word-of-mouth marketing. Many businesses have been built from the foundation of referrals from friends. Here are two examples of companies that established themselves based on customers spreading the word when they found a product they enjoyed.

Pinkberry

In 2005, Shelley Hwang and Young Lee opened a frozen yogurt shop in Los Angeles called Pinkberry. Word spread so quickly about the new, delicious frozen yogurt that people drove from all over Los Angeles to the small, West Hollywood store to get their yogurt fix. The *Los Angeles Times* article entitled, "The Taste that Launched 1,000 Parking Tickets" says it all. People didn't care that parking was tough in this tiny neighborhood. They were willing to risk the cost of a parking ticket to taste the tart, unique flavor of Pinkberry. In 2007, Howard Schultz's (of Starbucks fame) venture capital firm invested $27 million in Pinkberry.

Crocs

Another product that spread by word of mouth is Crocs. These rubber clogs are comfortable and waterproof, but distinctly different looking. Crocs began when three friends went on a boat trip and one of them wore a pair of foam clogs. Because of their extreme comfort, they decided to build a business around them. A grassroots word-of-mouth campaign began and all of sudden you would see a nicely dressed woman wearing Crocs. Everyone was wearing them. In 2003, Crocs' revenue was $1 million. In February 2006, Crocs went public with the initial offering of the company's stock. It had revenues that year more than $350 million. Who says talk is cheap?

Publicity

Once your product is ready to be sold in the marketplace, you need to generate publicity. Publicity takes many forms. It may be a YouTube video, an advertising campaign, or editorial coverage in a newspaper or magazine. The difference between marketing/publicity and editorial coverage is that marketing/publicity is often paid for in some fashion, whereas editorial is free attention generated from the press covering your product. At trade shows and on websites, many companies proudly display photos appearing in the pages of top lifestyle magazines. Your goal will be the same: to get free exposure from the popular consumer magazines that relate to your product. This exposure lends credibility to your product.

How to Use a Publicist

A publicist is a person whose job it is to generate publicity (also known as PR or public relations) for a variety of clients—companies, events, or celebrities, for example. Some publicists are independent contractors and work on their own out of a home office, while others work for public relations agencies. Public relations agencies sometimes specialize in one category, such as beauty, sports, technology, celebrity, or fashion.

Unless you have a big budget, you'll be your company's first publicist (along with all of the other titles you have). Publicists' monthly fees can range from $1,500 to $10,000 and up. You usually sign a contract for a minimum of six months. You can also find companies that handle public relations differently than a standard PR firm.

They work on a "performance" basis, meaning you only pay them if you get "placement" in a magazine or on a television show. Regular PR firms earn their monthly fee, whether or not any of their efforts have materialized.

In your search for a publicist, once again, ask for referrals from colleagues whose success with the press you admire. If that fails, use your industry's trade magazines to see if any firms place ads or are mentioned within articles. Or visit the Public Relations Society of America (*www.prsa.org*) and use their Membership Link to go into the Membership Directory to get to the PR Firms and Counselors list which takes you into the "Counselor Connect" search feature. Counselor Connect is the online directory of publicists who are members of their organization. You also want someone with a successful track record and established contacts and relationships within your market that they can call on immediately.

million-dollar TIP You cannot be guaranteed results from a publicist (no matter what he says). But you *can* have him list all the things he will do for you. Insist on specifics so you can hold him accountable for those tasks. Most public relations firms will tell you that it takes at least six months to generate their leads and see them in print, so if you can't afford to be patient, consider putting that money into your own grassroots campaign. You can do a lot of marketing for the cost of one month of public relations efforts that may turn up empty.

Work Successfully with a Publicist

If you decide to take on a publicist, be in close contact with her so you know she is working diligently on your behalf. Here are some tips for a successful partnership:

- Discuss in detail what she will be doing daily, weekly, and monthly. Ask for progress reports. Communicate frequently.

- Provide her with all your marketing materials so she can prepare a comprehensive press release and send out your materials to media outlets immediately. Give her your electronic images (logos, artwork, photos), your postcards, fliers, brochures, pricing lists, and anything else that might be useful.
- Find out exactly what is included in the monthly fee. Some publicists bill clients like law firms. They charge you for every phone call made on your behalf, every page they fax for you, every postal charge, etc. See what you can get included in your monthly fee. It's tough to get a bill full of miscellaneous items at the end of a month, especially if no coverage has materialized yet.
- Set goals together to be sure you want the same end result and that no one is duplicating efforts. Work with a publicist that understands and shares your vision. Meet monthly to review the status on those goals and make new ones.
- Ask her how you can help her efforts.
- Ask to be included in some meetings with media contacts if possible.

Publicists offer a great service, but it comes at a cost. Weigh your options and if you can't afford it now, consider it again later once you've got more cash. Or maybe you can barter this service.

Press Release

The first thing you need to generate publicity, whether you do it yourself or use a professional, is a formal press release. A press release is a written statement about your company and product, usually promoting something specific with a "hook," something that grabs the reader's attention. Press releases follow a specific format and are usually one page, double-spaced documents. You can put press releases in your press kit or send them to buyers via e-mail. You can also find services that will deliver your press release to a specific industry. Check out *www.prweb.com*, which offers different levels of services at reasonable prices.

To begin writing one yourself, include the following:

- Your company name
- An exciting and timely title to catch attention
- Description of what you are selling
- Your product's benefits
- Your contact information

Once you've assembled these, write an announcement that alerts everyone to the arrival of your product to the marketplace. Your story needs a unique angle, so that when it gets to an editor of a magazine, they're immediately intrigued. Consider what made you think of the idea in the first place, and see if you can parlay that into a headline that will grab the reader. Then begin your "story" by announcing the benefits of your product. Marketing Source offers a great sample template and more explanation of writing an effective press release at *www.marketingsource.com/pressrelease/releaseformat.html.*

If they can do it, *So Can you!*

Geek Squad founder Robert Stephens started his business in 1994 with $200 and a bicycle. He was a self-proclaimed computer geek and made house calls to solve computer problems. Robert began to add other "geeks" to his "squad" and built his brand by having the geeks arrive looking like "special agents." They all wear black pants, white shirts, and black ties. In 2004, Best Buy acquired Geek Squad and they work out of many Best Buy stores. Today, there are more than 15,000 "special agents" who can fix not only your computer but your iPod, television, and GPS systems, too.

Make Your Own Press Kit (also known as "Media Kit")

Press kits are packages of information and samples that you will send to buyers and to editors of magazines and trade papers. They make a complete presentation of your product and company.

Inside Press Kits

The typical contents are:

- Your press release (printed on company letterhead)
- An article from a trade magazine promoting the need for your product (if available)
- Your postcard
- A sample of the product or glossy photo
- Frequently Asked Questions (FAQ) sheet (if your product requires more explanation than a photo can offer). Cover the five most important selling points and eliminate any confusion.

If the kit is going to a buyer, you can also include a wholesale pricing list. Be sure those lists go *only to buyers*, however, not editors. If editors receive the wholesale list, they will quote that price to their readers instead of the actual marked-up retail cost (big problem!). Have a separate retail-pricing sheet available if requested by editors or anyone else that deals directly with consumers.

An inexpensive way to make a standard press kit is to use folders with pockets. You can find laminated two-pocket folders at any office supply store. Be sure they are laminated—that format is sturdy and has a nice, glossy finish. Customize the front of the folder with your company logo stickers. Be sure that each and every piece within your marketing package has your contact information. Include your name, company name, address, phone, fax, website address, and e-mail.

Once you have all the materials for your press kit together, assemble twenty-five to thirty. Initially, these kits will be sent to both buyers and editors, and you want to get a decent number out. You want to distribute these kits to anyone who needs one, so have stock on hand at all times. It's a real time-saver!

Build a Database of Magazine Editors

If you decide to do your own publicity, start a database of magazine editors, newspaper editors, and local television contacts. The easiest method for magazines is to buy an issue (as opposed to going to the website) and get the information from the magazine's "masthead" in the front of the magazine. This lists all the editors and the magazine's mailing address and phone number. Contact the main phone number and confirm that the editor you want is still the correct editor.

million-dollar **TIP** Monthly magazines often go to press much earlier than you might expect. Editors will need story ideas four to six months before the issue hits newsstands. Ask editors about their specific lead times and keep that information handy. Think far ahead about promotional opportunities. Don't wait until November to send out information on your holiday gift promotions. The November issue is being put together in spring/summer, when your thoughts are not on Christmas yet. Have a calendar where you can remind yourself of editorial deadlines.

Take the time to understand the magazine's audience and content and make sure you can pitch your product with a hook that will pique the interest of an editor. Be persistent! Keep the mailings going to these editors with a fresh story every eight weeks or so. The editorial departments of many magazines are located in New York City, so if you have a chance to go there at some point, you could try to make appointments to visit several editors in one day, making a personal introduction and bringing samples if possible. For example, Condé Nast (*www.condenast.com*) is one of the largest magazine publishing companies and under their one roof are all the following magazines: *Vogue, GQ, Glamour, Allure, Self, Details, Architectural Digest, Modern Bride, Domino, Cookie, Lucky, Golf Digest, Vanity Fair, Gourmet, Bon Appétit, Condé Nast Traveler,* and *Wired.* Editors are very busy, however, so don't be disappointed if you can't get a face-to-face meeting.

Advanced Marketing Ideas

Once you've completed the basic round of marketing and publicity and your product gains sales momentum and success, consider some of these fun and potentially profitable opportunities. You could try these things earlier in the process, of course—weigh your options based on your chance of success, the time you need to invest in it, and how much money you have to play with. And as always, let your product and its audience lead the way.

Philanthropy

A great way to get your product out there while doing good is to align your company with a cause that you feel strongly about, and donate a portion of your proceeds to that charitable organization. People may feel an emotional tie to your company because of this generosity. You see these words on many products in today's marketplace: "A portion of our proceeds go to. . . ." This is also known as "social entrepreneurship." Many large and small companies worldwide have successfully aligned themselves with a philanthropic cause.

Start by choosing an organization with a cause that means something to you. If there is a women's shelter you would like to donate to, give them a call. Since you will probably not be giving large donations at first, it may feel more meaningful to start with a local cause that would appreciate even small donations. Let the group know that you appreciate their work and would like to help in a small way by donating a small percentage (which you will determine) of your profits to their organization. Then it is up to you to write the check on a regular basis—quarterly or semiannually, for example.

You can also discuss the possibility of using their logo on some of your marketing materials so that customers are aware that you support a cause that is within their own community or something that they may feel strongly about as well.

If they can do it, *So Can You!*

One of the most famous success stories tied to philanthropy is Ethos Water. Founder Peter Thum was distraught after visiting South Africa and seeing firsthand the lack of safe drinking water available. He wanted to help fix the problem, so he decided to sell premium bottled water and donate a percentage of profits to people in need of clean water. Ethos's philanthropic concept touched Howard Schultz, CEO of Starbucks. He loved the idea and bought the company. Ethos is both profitable and charitable—a great combination!

Private Label Marketing Opportunities

Many companies look to outside sources to create products they don't make themselves for a variety of reasons, but they want to sell under their brand name. Rather than thinking that you should sell your idea to one of these larger companies, instead try to become a manufacturing source for them. You have probably seen this before but have not even noticed it as such. For example, high-end fashion designer Isaac Mizrahi designs an affordable line of clothing available only at Target. The key to maintaining your brand name is to include it somewhere on the product, by labeling it with a tag saying, "Made for Company A by Company B," just as Mizrahi does. Moisture Jamzz has been able to benefit from private labeling while still maintaining exposure for our brand name by having the inner labels read "Moisture Jamzz for Bath & Body Works," for example. This business-to-business marketing is very lucrative. Once your product becomes part of their line, you benefit from their established market share and all of a sudden, you have a new audience in their large customer base.

How to Approach a Big Corporation about Private Labeling

Find a company or retailer where your product would fit in perfectly with their merchandise. If they only sell items under their own brand name, you need to:

1. Figure out a system of private labeling that will work for your product. For example, if you sell the best all-natural soy candles and you want to private label them for a big name spa, talk with your graphic artist about creating other artwork to complement another company's brand image on your packaging. Your graphic designer could start by making a flier that shows your product(s) with the words "Put Your Logo Here" on your packaging. The package should look generic so buyers are not distracted by your artwork and design.

    If a company is interested, your designer can take the company's actual logo either from a product that you buy or sometimes from their website and make a mockup that shows what you can do exclusively for their company brand. This mockup will immediately feel like a customized product and makes it easier for the buyer to see how it could fit right into their line.

Send the generic fliers out to prospective private label clients and have them available to hand out at trade shows.

2. Call the company's corporate headquarters and try to locate the appropriate contact. Asking for someone in "merchandising" or "new product development" should lead you to the right person within their corporate structure.

3. When you have reached the right contact, ask if he would be interested in learning about your product (or line) and discussing private label opportunities. If he says yes, but nothing further, have your graphic artist make that sample mockup quickly.

4. Put a press kit together with the sample and send it off. Remind him that the mockup is rough and the final product would have the quality and finish that they expect. Include any testimonials about your product and any press material (if your product has been featured in a magazine editorial) that you have. If a company is going to put its name on your product, they will need to be sure it is going to be up to par with the quality their customers expect. This is a serious partnership and you will need to prove yourself to the buyer.

5. Follow up with the buyer and ask the following questions: Do you see the product as a nice addition to your current offerings? Would you want an exclusive on either the fragrance or the size, shape, or color (meaning, that particular style will not be sold anywhere else)? What else can I make for you as a product extension utilizing our specialties?

6. Find a way to meet their demand by talking to your manufacturer, designer, and packaging source. It might be beneficial to put your graphic artist directly in touch with them to discuss the design specifics, especially for technological reasons. Keep communication lines open by letting the account know you can customize as much as they would like.

7. You will most likely be producing in larger quantities than your usual run. Expect that they will ask for a discount, even on a custom order. You should be receiving discounts from your manufacturer because of the larger quantities you're ordering, so it should even out in the end.

The key goal of your marketing efforts is to make your product stand out from its competition. Have professional-looking marketing materials, a strong online presence, and be organized and diligent in your strategy. Find your niche and make the most of it.

When you've completed these steps, buyers and consumers will see your business as a "real company." So long as your product can deliver what you promise, it won't make any difference that behind the façade is an excited entrepreneur in pajamas at the kitchen table anxiously waiting for an order!

find and sell to buyers

Flaming enthusiasm, backed up by horse sense and persistence, is the quality that most frequently makes for success.

—DALE CARNEGIE

Sometimes a buyer is just a phone call away. Other times, it seems like you're trying to get through to the President at the White House. It can be intimidating to approach a buyer, but remember that this is what you've been working toward. Buyers will help get your product in front of consumers. The keys to winning them over are having a great product, filling a void in their offering, and being easy to work with and reliable. You can do all that, right? Let's look at some common scenarios and selling tactics.

Basic Industry Lingo

Before talking with any buyers, familiarize yourself with the lingo of your particular industry as well as the lingo buyers use regarding purchasing options and terms. Buyers can talk fast and if they ask you a question about a purchase order and you respond with silence, it could be a deal breaker. To avoid that, be familiar with these common terms for retail dealings:

- **Doors** is another name for a physical store. If you are launching a new makeup line with Neiman Marcus and they are only "testing" it in ten stores to see how it will sell before selling it in more stores, the buyer may say something like, "We are testing you in ten doors and will roll you out to more if the line is successful."

- **F.O.B.** stands for freight on board. It refers to the city from where you ship out the product and where they will be paying freight from. A buyer may ask, "Where's your FOB?" You would say, "Our FOB is Los Angeles or whatever city you ship from.

- An **invoice** is the sales document that you send to the accounts payable department of the company that ordered from you. It is a detailed account of each item shipped, its corresponding item number, and price. You might say, "We will send the invoice separate from the shipment. It will go to your accounting department." Office and electronic stores offer a variety of popular software programs that can help you create, send, and manage your invoices. Here are a few: *www.quicken.com, www.peachtree.com*, and *www.intuit.com.*

- **Lead time** refers to the amount of time it takes for you to ship an order out. A buyer may ask, "What is the lead time on 1,000 units?" You could respond, "Our lead time right now is about seven to ten days." Or, in a proposal, you could say, "Please allow two to four weeks lead time on your initial order."

- A **packing slip** should be sent with each shipment. A packing slip lists exactly what is in the shipment and the number of cartons in the total shipment. It is usually inside a small envelope that is stuck to the outside of the box. Packing slip envelopes are sold at office supply stores.

- **PO** stands for purchase order. Receiving POs is the name of the game. A purchase order contains the order placed by the buyer. A buyer may say, "I am issuing the PO next week" or "The PO number is 1234."

Components of a PO
- Buyer's name
- Carrier preference
- Company's name, phone number, ship to and bill to addresses

- Date issued
- Date to either be delivered by or cancelled if not delivered by
- Price and quantity of items ordered
- Pricing terms
- Their item number
- Total PO amount
- UPC number
- Your product(s) name and item number
- Your vendor number

Some purchase orders from smaller stores may include nothing more than the store name, address, contact information, quantities, item name, price, and terms.

- **Sales reps** are representatives that sell many product brands directly to retailers. Reps usually work within a specialty market. For example, they would represent many beauty products (makeup, candles, soaps, perfumes) or sell lines of home accents (pillows, bedding, lamps, tables). They have contacts within that specific market who trust the reps to bring in quality products that are new and innovative. Some retailers like buying from rep groups because they can find many products from one source and place one order for all of the lines.

  You could decide to have a rep try to sell your products to some of your markets. A rep usually works on a 15 percent commission of the gross amount of the purchase order. If your rep writes a $500 order for your products, she will earn $75 on the sale. They have accounts that they regularly call upon within a specific territory and they try to add your line to those retailers.

- The term "**ship via**" means the method by which you will ship the goods. The bigger companies will tell *you* which carrier to use. They usually have an account with a freight or trucking company. If this is the case, you will ship via their requested carrier and not bill them for the cost because they are billed directly from the carrier. The PO will say "Ship Via" and they will fill in UPS or Acme Trucking or their preferred company's name. If the company leaves that up to you, you will pick the best rate and carrier and you will bill them for the cost of the UPS/FedEx shipment. You might say, "We will ship via UPS and bill you for freight."

- **SKU** (Stock Keeping Unit) is the number used to identify the product within a store. It may or may not be seen by the customer. It could be an internal stock keeping number used to identify the product, price, and manufacturer. If a buyer asks you, "How many SKUs do you have?" you will respond with the number of products that you offer because each product would be assigned a different SKU number. If you offer one product in ten different designs, you have ten SKUs. Each new variance and design will be issued a different bar code or SKU number. See *www.gs1us.org* for a helpful tutorial by clicking their "Quick Links" topic called Bar Codes and eCom. The FAQ section is also helpful: Under the "About" link, go into the GS1 link.

- **Terms** refers to payment terms and when you will be paid on an order that has shipped. A standard term is "Net 30," which means they will pay you thirty days after the company receives your product. Some companies try to stretch it out to Net 45 or Net 60. Try to always have Net 30—you'll get paid faster! You can also offer even more specific terms, such as 2% Net 10, meaning they save 2 percent if they pay within ten days.

  If you are able to accept credit cards, mom-and-pop accounts can pay that way, but be prepared to eat the small fee from the credit card company. Sometimes, it is worth the small fee to get your hands on the money in advance of thirty days. A buyer may say, "We work on Net 30 terms." A small account may inquire, "What are your terms?" You could say, "We work on Net 30 and we also accept credit cards."

- **UPC** (Universal Product Code) codes (also known as "SKUs") are found on every product in the form of scannable bars. (We touched on this in Step 5.)

- A **vendor** is a company that sells goods. If you are selling products to Bed, Bath & Beyond stores, you are a Bed, Bath & Beyond vendor. If the Bed, Bath & Beyond buyer agrees to sell your product there, she may say something like, "We will set you up in the system as a new vendor."

Now that you know the lingo, let's talk about sales calls.

If you find out that a particular buyer no longer works at an account you're trying to land, don't be discouraged. Ask to speak with his replacement. If you can get the buyer on the phone or find his e-mail address, ask if he was given the media kit from the previous buyer. If it was not passed on, send a new one to the current buyer and start fresh.

Mom-and-Pop Stores

Mom-and-pop stores are the most approachable businesses for your new product, so they're a good place to start.

How to Approach Them

Call the store directly and ask for the buyer's name. Simple! Send a press kit and a sample if possible. Follow-up is just as easy—the phone is usually answered by a real live person and the buyer will almost always listen to a pitch. If they are local, ask to set up an appointment and just go in for the pitch. Begin a relationship. If the product isn't right at the moment, ask if you can call her back in a month or two and keep her posted on your new information. Start a database of the companies you have approached so you remember who you spoke with, when, and what he or she said.

Small but Powerful

While these small accounts may not bring in much money with each order, if they become regular, their monthly or bimonthly orders will add up and can last years or even decades. Small accounts are also loyal customers. Typically, if your product sells well for them, they will want to bring in more of your brand. Mom-and-pop accounts also provide security, especially when you have built up hundreds of these smaller accounts. If one (or a few) closes, you still have many others buying from you. When you have a big chain buyer, yes, the account is huge and the checks are big, but the chain can change direction or find a competing source and can end the relationship at any minute, devastatingly affecting your bottom line. So treasure the small accounts too!

Test Products There

You can also use mom-and-pop stores as a market research testing field. Market testing is also useful after you've established a good relationship and sales history. You can bring in a few final versions of a new product, offer it at a very low discount if they are reluctant to buy it at first, and see how they sell. You may learn valuable feedback (mom-and-pop owners are usually very knowledgeable about what their customers like) before taking the product to larger chains.

Big Chain Stores

Dealing with large chain stores is a vastly different experience. It can be very difficult to even find out who the buyer is for a specific department.

How to Approach Them

If you have a new kitchen accessory and you think it should be sold in Williams-Sonoma, call its corporate buying office and ask for the name of the buyer for your product. Unfortunately, you will probably not get the name of the buyer. That is pretty much standard operating procedure with the big chains. They simply don't want to give names out because they do not want their buyers hounded by people like you and me. They have other work to do and there are lots of us out there. Instead, they may transfer you to an announcement of how they would like new vendors to submit their products. When you have to send a package to the attention of "New Vendor Submission" or "Accessories Buyer" because you don't have a name, it is pretty much impossible to follow up with anyone. So, you have to find creative ways to break down the barrier and get more specific contact information.

Tips for Getting Past Corporate Red Tape

Here's a secret way I have found to get a buyer's name (though once this gets out, there may be a new phone system that won't allow "hackers" like me). When you call the corporate buying office and the phone system answers: "You have reached the Big Company's corporate office. If you know your party's extension, you may dial it at anytime. If you would like a dial-by-name directory, please press 1." Press 1. Then it usually says, "If you know your party's last name, please dial the first three letters of the person's last name followed by the pound sign." Dial SMI, for Smith, a very common name. Then you will be told the names of the people who match that entry. If there isn't anyone, try another name combination (HAR for Harris is also common). Keep trying until you get a list of names in response.

You will hear something like "Would you like Tom Smith or Mary Smitson?" Press the extension number for either. When Mary or Tom pick up their line, say, "Oh, I must have the wrong extension, I am looking for the kitchen accessory buyer, can you connect me or just give me their e-mail address?" Once you are connected, you'll either get that person on the phone (people will usually answer with his or her name) or you will hear the name on the voice mail message. This technique often works because the person who initially answered is busy and wants to end the call. Funny enough, but this has worked like a charm for me many times.

With some companies, however, you don't have any other choice but to send your product to the generic buyer (Men's Buyer, Women's Buyer, Accessories Buyer) and keep your fingers crossed. I have received both rejection letters and purchase orders when I've sent packages to generic buyers, so it pays to send one even if you cannot get a name.

Some large corporations will not give you the buyer's name but will transfer you to the buying department, where you can speak to a receptionist. Have your fifteen- to thirty-second pitch summarizing your product ready to go. Also, ask to whose attention your package with samples should be sent.

The conversation should go something like this: *"Hi, my name is Joe with Joe's New Kitchen Products. We designed an incredible new kitchen utensil that is unique and perfect for parents with young children. It fits right into your kitchen department and I would like to send our press kit and sample to the appropriate buyer. Could you please give me the contact name?"* Ask for the correct spelling of the name and if it is Ms. or Mr. You obviously do not want to send a package to Mr. Joe Wood if Jo is actually Joanna Wood. Also, confirm the mailing address and review spelling from their website.

Follow Up

Try not to speak with the buyer until you are sure he received the package. (If you send the package by UPS or FedEx, you can track it online for confirmation.) Once you see that it has been delivered, follow up with a phone call a few days later. If he tells you he hasn't received it, it could be because their offices are large and the package is being processed by a mailroom or because he just hasn't opened it.

If you get the "not received yet" response, mention that you see it was delivered and signed for by J. Doe, but that you would be happy to call back in another day or so. Give a quick pitch too, like, "You are going to love this new, unique design that we have for this utensil. I look forward to talking with you after you have seen the package." With luck, the buyer will say, "Okay, call me on Friday. I should have looked at it by then."

Or, the buyer may say "Yes, Joe, I received the package but I am in the middle of a big project. I will have to get back to you." I like to say, "Absolutely, we can talk later. Would it be all right if I make a note to call you again on the thirtieth?" Then you have "permission" to call him back. Sometimes he will even begin to talk a bit right then because he can see you are polite and not nudging. Always accommodate his requests for time and don't be pushy or aggressive.

How to Respond to the "No, Thanks" Rejection

If a buyer has received and reviewed your package, you could get a number of responses, one of which is negative. The key is to be prepared so you can respond nicely to any negative comments. Always try to find out exactly why they are not interested. Politely pump the buyer for information by doing the following:

- Ask what you could do differently to make your product a better fit for her stores.
- Is it a single feature about the product that she doesn't like? For example, is the packaging or pricing holding her back? See if you can change something that will alleviate this concern for her. You may not be able to solve the problem immediately, but you could try work out some alternatives.
- Keep a dialogue going. If you keep resolving their problems with your product, eventually you may receive the purchase order.
- Take action. Listen to the objections carefully and find solutions. For example, if the issue was that the packaging needed to be different, call your graphic artist and ask for a new package design in the correct format. Have your artist send it to you electronically so you can send it to the buyer, saying, "You had requested this type of packaging. We can easily package it this way for you. How do you feel about this design?"

Preplanned Responses

Review these common reasons a buyer may give when he rejects your product. Write your response. After this exercise, you'll always be prepared to quickly state your answer to their issues.

POSSIBLE REJECTIONS	YOUR WAY TO OVERCOME IT
Packaging isn't right for our store.	We can easily change that. . . .
The price is too high.	We can offer incentive discounts on first few orders.
Not sure how to display.	We can add hang tabs or provide a stand.
Already carry a similar product.	Our line is really different, because. . . .

Persistence Pays Off

It may take you months or even years to get orders from some stores. It took me *four years* to land a particular chain store where I knew my gloves would fit in perfectly. I kept sending updated packages every four months, and the buyer kept rejecting me when I called to follow up. Then, one day I heard words that were music to my ears. The receptionist said, "That buyer no longer works here." Yippee! I was jumping up and down in my bedroom, er, office. I asked for the name of the new buyer and sent her a package. It turns out that she had bought our gloves at a competitor's store and loved them. They are still a client today, ten years later.

So, you never know. Sometimes you have to wait for a buyer to move on, and they do, occasionally. On the other hand, even if the buyer does not change, sometimes it takes time and hard work to land an account. Maybe the buyer wants to see if your company is still around in several months. He may not want to do business with a brand-new company if he is going to place a substantial order. Also, maybe they need to wait for "buzz" to surround your product, which you can get from your marketing and publicity efforts. If you get good word-of-mouth advertising going, customers may even begin to request your product. If you truly believe your product and the store are a match, be persistent. Not annoying—just persistent.

If they can do it, *So Can You!*

When Estée Lauder was launching her perfume, she met with the buyer for a department store. The buyer rejected the perfume. As she left the cosmetics area, she intentionally spilled drops of her perfume so the entire area smelled of her perfume. People liked the scent so much they began asking for it. The buyer had to call and order. "No" doesn't have to mean "no." Try creative responses.

TV Shopping Channels

Getting your product featured on a shop-at-home television channel such as QVC and the Home Shopping Network can be a dream come true for a start-up company. These channels sell products around the clock and have made household names out of many makeup artists', clothing designers', and hairstylists 'lines.

Dream big and pursue QVC—it is known for launching small, unique items sold on air directly by the inventor. According to their website, "QVC reaches approximately 166 million homes worldwide." If you think your product would be fantastic on one of the home shopping channels, but you don't want to actually appear on television, don't worry! You can find companies that have trained "on-air personalities" who will sell your product for you, for a fee or percentage of sales.

Here are a few methods for getting your product considered for a TV spot:

- **Watch the shows and determine where your product could fit into one of their segments.** Then send a press kit much like you did to other media, but tailor it to a specific show and explain how the product would mesh well.
- **Look for special events.** For example, sometimes QVC offers "Product Searches" in a variety of cities around the United States. You can bring your product to one of these events and get immediate feedback from a buyer. Visit *www.qvcproductsearch.com* for upcoming dates.
- **Go online.** Both HSN (*www.hsn.com*, click on "Become an HSN Partner") and QVC (*www.qvc.com*, click on "Vendor Relations") accept online product submissions.
- **Emphasize that you're an inventor.** Home shopping channels love featuring the "inventor"—it offers their audience a chance to connect with the people behind the products they purchase.

- **Attend industry trade shows.** Home shopping channels often send buyers to scout out new products.
- **Use a sales rep.** You can find sales reps who sell to every part of an industry, including home shopping channels. They often know the buyers and represent many product lines. Consider using one of these reps if you're too busy to do it yourself or if you feel you could use someone with insider knowledge. Interview a sales rep like you would any other professional—get referrals, recommendations, and review his or her past successes.

Catalogs and Online-Only Stores

These two outlets sort of fall into the same category because you're dealing with selling your product via words and pictures only—the consumer can't pick it up and touch it. That said, people spend billions of dollars a year buying products online and in catalogs, so these are important outlets. Be sure to search out catalogs—you'll likely find many you have never seen before. Another tip: Some catalogs that are attached to department stores offer items in the catalog that are not carried in the stores. So don't rule out the catalog buyer if you get rejected by the in-store buyer.

Selling to catalogs is sometimes a bit easier because they are usually smaller operations, so you have a better chance of locating a specific buyer. Also, catalogs usually have a specific retail focus and therefore fewer buyers than at a big chain store.

Of course, not all catalog buyers will be easy to reach. Some will give you the same runaround as the chain stores, so you may have to send your press kit to a generic department or buyer. If you have to go that route, follow-up is pretty impossible; you have to either wait for the rejection letter or a positive response (usually in the mail or occasionally e-mailed within four to six weeks).

It's tough to generalize about selling to online-only stores (such as *www.amazon.com* and *www.zappos.com*). They're still a relatively new industry and differ widely in their operations. If you're interested in getting your product on an online store, search the site for their "new vendors" link. If that fails, call their customer service line or e-mail their general e-mail address and see if they can help you.

Closing the Deal

A sale is not made the minute a buyer shows interest in your product. Learn some basic sales tactics to give your product its best shot. Consider checking out some short, inexpensive, and helpful beginner salesperson guides, such as *Closing Techniques (That Really Work!)* by Stephan Schiffman. You'll find some immediately useful tactics to help you prepare for a meeting with a buyer.

Above all, keep in mind that a buyer's job is to find and purchase products that will sell in her stores or her particular department. Buyers are not in the business of making friends and they are very busy. They may not be as available as you'd like or have time to hear the story of how your idea came to life. Don't get discouraged! Keep thinking of ways to get through the barriers and work around obstacles. Be creative, be professional, and be persistent.

Incentives

Sometimes a buyer likes your product but seems on the fence about actually writing a purchase order (PO). When this happens, have an arsenal of incentives you can offer to close the sale. Here are a few ideas.

Incentives for Closing a Sale
- Offer a discount—know ahead of time what you can work with, say, 5 percent to 20 percent.
- Offer free shipping on their initial order.
- Offer longer-than-usual payment terms (for example, Net 45 instead of Net 30).
- Offer a return policy (if the product doesn't sell, the account can return it for a full or partial refund).

Try not to make these incentives sound like a desperate attempt to make a sale. In other words, don't beg. Approach it as a win-win solution—he gets product to sell at an arrangement he's comfortable with, and you make a sale. Before you offer the kitchen sink, ask what's holding up the sale. It may be a more minor issue than you expected, such as timing—and one that you can address without sacrificing profit.

How Much Does the Buyer Have to Purchase?

Most companies that sell wholesale have a minimum order quantity required to place an order. For example, Moisture Jammz has a reasonable $120 minimum first-time wholesale order amount (which equates to twenty-four pairs of our gloves or socks). At that price, it's not a huge investment for a new client to try our line. Honestly, $120 is about as low as you should go for a minimum order, and don't go higher than $500 on products that have a low wholesale cost (say, from $5 to $20). For some small mom-and-pop stores, ordering a new product and having to pay anything more than $125 for an initial buy may seem like too big a risk. If you have costly opening minimums, it gives the impression that you don't want to work with smaller stores. The bottom line: Try to be flexible. Don't turn away business.

If you feel a buyer is gauging her risk, ask her what it would take for her to place an order. I know, it sounds like a car salesperson line. But even though it's a cliché, the question puts the ball in her court and requires a direct answer. It's especially useful at trade shows where you need to close the sale when the buyer is standing in your booth. Try to make an arrangement that suits the buyer and where she feels there is little risk in purchasing. For instance, if she's unsure her clientele will buy your product, offer her a thirty-day full refund policy. If she says the opening order is too large, offer a discount. Do whatever it takes (within reason, of course) to get the new account.

Don't Give Up

You need to be creative and resourceful first to locate buyers, and then to convince these buyers to offer your new product to their customers. Keep new angles and new information coming to the buyer. Know the fine line between being persistent and being an annoyance. Sometimes you need to step back and give the buyer time to hear the buzz about your company, see your product in a competitor's store, or just think about it and try your samples out.

million-dollar TIP As you begin selling, you'll find you have less time for administrative tasks. When you have some profit coming in, consider hiring someone to do tasks you don't have to do yourself, such as assembling press kits, packing orders for shipment, filing paperwork, or entering database information. Make a concerted effort never to sacrifice time spent trying to sell because you are doing the busy work.

Electronic Purchase Orders

Of course, purchase orders have kept up with the times and are now often filed electronically, especially by larger chain stores. They use what's called EDI (electronic data interchange), which is a paperless system that allows buyers and sellers to exchange business documents such as purchase orders, invoices, and shipping information. Instead of faxing or mailing documents, more than 100,000 businesses use EDI today. It's fast, efficient, and computerized, so there are fewer human errors and delays.

How It Works

If you sell to a chain store that utilizes this method, you have to get on board in order to do business with them. They will instruct you on how to follow their particular system and they will recommend preferred partners to work with. They will likely have an EDI

Keep a Buyer Contact Log

It is critical to keep track of your last conversation with the buyer. Put all communication in the log, even e-mails and voice mails. Set aside an entire page per buyer or use a word processing or spreadsheet program on your computer so you have plenty of space. Keep meticulous notes, because you may begin to forget details as you begin to speak with lots of buyers.

Start some blank pages set up like the following:

COMPANY NAME	Big Huge Company
BUYER	James Sims
TITLE	Accessories Buyer
PHONE	555-555-1212
E-MAIL	jsims@bighuge.com

June 20: Sent press kit

June 27: James said he had not yet received, re-call Fri June 30.

June 30: James likes product, bringing to his meeting July 15. Re-call July 16.

July 16: Associates like it, they want pricing proposal for the new forks at 2,500, 5,000, and 10,000 units.

July 17: Sent proposal, follow up July 20.

July 20: They will purchase 10,000. Purchase order will be faxed in a week.

department to assist you if you need help. Here are two common methods of using EDI:

1. The EDI is made available through the company itself and costs nothing to join and has no monthly fee. Obviously, this option is great, but it's rare.
2. You use a third-party web-based EDI facilitator. These companies provide all the software, forms, and support for a monthly fee, a one-time set-up fee, and/or a flat fee for a certain number of transactions or a cost-per-transaction fee. The fees will vary from company to company, but you may see an average of a $500 one-time set-up fee for the first trading partner (you can add other retailers if required to do so for $100) and a monthly fee of around $75 to $120, including, say, 150 transactions.

A typical EDI transaction includes the PO, the invoice, and the shipping information. Here are some companies that make using EDI easy: *www.covalentworks.com*, *www.truecommerce.com,* and *www.inovis.com*. Some companies will let you sign up on a month-to-month basis rather than a long-term contract. Your online account will alert you via e-mail if you have new purchase orders, so you don't have to constantly check in to be sure that you don't miss anything. You can process the documents online, by filling in the blanks on the form, confirming receipt, and then electronically sending an invoice back to your account upon shipping the order.

How to Deal with Buyers

If a buyer of a large chain store asks you if you are EDI compatible, say "not at the moment, but we can certainly set that up right away for you." (Keep in mind that it usually takes a week or so to get set up and do the required testing by the retailer.) The next step would be to register with a web-based EDI service. Sign up according to the specifics from your retail partner.

Once you fill out the forms a few times, you get used to it. Like e-mail, it's fast, efficient, and you can access it from anywhere.

Before you sign up for EDI, ask the buyer if his order is just a "testing" of your product. If so, it will most likely be too costly to set up EDI, so ask if they could just fax the initial testing orders. Then say that if they proceed to actually add your line in more stores, you will implement EDI.

How to Fill Orders

When you receive a purchase order via EDI, fax, e-mail, or phone, celebrate your accomplishment. Congratulations! Your next steps will be:

1. Note the purchase order in a log so you can keep track of orders (when they are issued, shipped, and invoiced). This system will help you monitor how often certain accounts order so you can better manage your inventory. Confirm receipt of the order and let them know when you will ship.
2. Physically fill the order—pull it from your inventory and recheck to be sure it is correctly filled before moving on.
3. Use your software program to create an invoice. Send the invoice separately by mail or e-mail.
4. Prepare the packing slip (which details the contents of the shipment). Put it in its envelope and tape it to the box.
5. Pack the order in the box. Be sure you have all necessary delivery information on the box.
6. Ship it. Either your carrier will pick it up at your "office," or you will mail it, with delivery confirmation so that it's trackable.
7. Get paid, either by credit card or check if the account is on Net 30 terms.

As your business takes off, fulfilling orders will become second nature to you. And with luck, you'll become so big an operation that you need a warehouse to do it for you.

Follow Up

The unofficial eighth step for fulfilling orders is to follow up on the account, especially if it's a large account. Just because you've shipped the order doesn't mean you're done with your end of the bargain. Make the most of the account; offer great customer service. Here are some ways to do that:

- If your product would be good for in-store promos (like makeup demonstrations or taste tasting), ask if you can do one in your area or at a high-volume store.
- Keep on top of the big accounts and be proactive if sales aren't what you were hoping. See if you can find out what the problem may be and offer a solution. For example, when Moisture Jamzz Moisture Gloves were sold through a very large chain and we weren't getting reorders from a particular region as quickly as usual, we went to look at those stores (or in some cases, we asked friends or family to look in their cities). We found that those locations had our gloves almost hidden in bins. The other stores had them hanging on hooks in plain view. We asked our buyer for help in getting them out of the bins. As soon as that happened, they sold swiftly again.

million-dollar TIP

If a customer is late in paying, it's okay to speak up. If it's a small account and the owner of a store placed the order, call that person and let him know that you are checking on "the status of a past-due invoice" ("open invoice" sounds less harsh, but the point is that it is late). Then provide the purchase order number, the invoice number, the amount due, and the date shipped. He will let you know if he already sent the check or he will cut the check right away. If it's a larger chain, ask to speak to accounts payable. Or you could always e-mail or fax the past due invoice with a note saying the same.

- While you don't want to nag the buyer, you can follow up and ask if sales are meeting her expectations. If they're not, brainstorm a way to help. Again, you don't want to be a pest, but if you can offer realistic, viable options, the buyer may want to hear them. If sales are exceeding expectations, that's wonderful but also another opportunity to offer your help (and a new sales pitch for more units or more of your line).

Special Shipping Situations

While many small accounts will only need their items packed and shipped with your carrier's label (and packing slip), others will have more elaborate demands. Here are two you may encounter.

Routing Guides for Large Accounts

Your larger accounts will usually have shipping or routing guidelines that detail their expectations for how product will arrive in their warehouses. You must follow their instructions or be charged fees for mistakes. You can even be charged for seemingly small mistakes, like not putting the UPC in the exact corner spot on the outer carton. Many stores require a lot of information on an outer box label. Be sure to double- and triple-check before sending out these kinds of packages.

Department stores are notorious for having extremely detailed shipping and labeling instructions and then meticulously reviewing for compliance. Some people think they generate substantial revenue from vendor chargebacks for the mistakes. While it can be a pain, be sure to follow the instructions. Not doing so only costs you money and potentially a lucrative account. Most stores ask for all the information in a certain way so they can properly and quickly distribute and sell your product. The last thing you want is for any silly mistakes to prevent them from doing that.

Shipping to a Distribution Center vs. Individual Stores

When you land a large account that has hundreds of stores, you will find two shipping options:

1. You ship to their distribution center and then they ship to their individual locations (this is the best).
2. You ship directly to each store.

If you ship to each store rather than the central distribution center, it costs more for shipping, of course, and for labor and time as well. This is where your wholesale license comes in handy—you'll need to buy a *lot* of shipping supplies. It is so much easier to ship to one central distribution center, but unfortunately you don't have a choice. Be sure you are 100 percent clear on the directions the store gives you before shipping anything out.

The Golden Rules of Customer Service

High-quality and attentive customer service goes a long way to ensuring long-term, meaningful business relationships with your accounts, both big and small. Customer service is the way you treat your customers—how you handle their inquiries, their complaints, and their orders. A customer that is always right is always a customer.

Treat Your Clients with Respect

As you probably know from personal experience, companies don't always treat customers with respect. Be better than that. Go out of your way to be accommodating, friendly, and efficient by doing the following:

- Provide a quality product.
- Be friendly. Even if you're having a rough day, take a deep breath and put on a happy face for your customers.

- Listen carefully to customer's praise and problems.
- Be grateful. Sincerely thank people for their orders.

Set a higher standard than what most people experience in today's high-tech, nonpersonal buying marketplace. I've found that people really appreciate personal touches. Recently, a customer wanted to have our products sent as a gift to her mother. She asked if we could write a card to include inside the package. We accommodated all her requests. It took us only a few minutes but she was so glad that we took care of it without hesitating.

Process Orders Efficiently

When you receive a purchase order via fax, e-mail, or phone, be sure to confirm receipt of the order within twenty-four hours, give a shipping estimate, and thank the client for their business. Whenever possible (likely for small accounts or individual shoppers), try to ship out your product within twenty-four hours of receipt of order. That prompt service shows the client you're grateful and efficient.

Customers also want the package to arrive in good shape. Take pride in your shipping services as well; be sure the package is packed properly. If you have to resend a package that was damaged, it inconveniences the customer and becomes costly for you, so do it right the first time. Unless your products are costly, don't ask the customer to send back damaged or defective items, just trust them and resend the order.

Listen to Your Customers' Praise— and Their Problems, Too!

Customer service also includes listening to your customers and resolving issues politely and calmly, no matter the nature of the customer's complaint.

These complaints usually come by phone or via e-mail. The key to resolving the issue is satisfying the customer. That is the goal, plain and simple. Make them feel that they are right and apologize for the problem (or inconvenience or mistake) on your part. Replace the product if necessary, refund the money if needed, but always resolve the issue in favor of the customer. Hopefully, she will then speak positively about your company and not spread negative comments either online or through conversations with friends.

I know what you're thinking—what if the customer is *not* right? What if the description online *did* say the color was navy blue, not sky blue? Well, there's nothing you can do. Take a deep breath, apologize that the color wasn't what the customer expected, and resolve the issue. If you're thorough and clear in your marketing materials and website and have a great quality product, you probably won't hear complaints too often.

Also, monitor relevant blogs and user reviews for people who complain about your product, but not directly to you. That's worse! Though you never *want* to hear from an angry customer, it's better to know he has a problem so you can do something to fix it and stop the negative word-of-mouth in its tracks. If you find a poor review or negative blog posting, see if that person's e-mail address is listed and contact him politely and try to resolve the situation. If not, "listen" to the complaint anyway and see if you can avoid that particular problem in the future.

People Love Giveaways

It's always nice to get a little something extra, isn't it? Spread the goodwill with your product. When shipping to individuals or to small mom-and-pop accounts, throw in anything from a promotional pen to a sample of something new in your line. Sample-size freebies are a win-win situation—the customer gets an extra surprise, and if she likes it, she may order a full size, thereby increasing your profits.

How Can Your Customer Service Stand Out?

Come up with ideas that will be inexpensive to implement but will offer something above and beyond what the competition offers. If you can solve a problem that other vendors ignore, you will be serving the customer well. Let your customers know it will benefit them to do business with you—how easy you make it, how there's no risk for them with your great return policy, how you value the time and money they invest when purchasing your brand. Stand behind your products with confidence, and the customer will feel good about buying from you as opposed to a competitor that offers nothing more than the usual.

The gift makes the customer feel special and helps build brand loyalty (the customer feels like she got something for free and she will order again, hoping for the same little perk). Sometimes people even take the time to say thanks because they are so surprised to get a freebie.

At Moisture Jamzz, we even try to personalize the freebie by keeping track of past orders. For example, if a client seems to always order only gloves, we will put in a complimentary pair of socks with a note saying, "Save 10 percent on your initial order of socks." With large orders we may send some extra product for the buyer (think before you send, however—if you're shipping to a distribution center or to individual stores in a large chain, the buyer may not work out of any of those places) or offer free shipping on orders over a certain dollar amount. Make it a company policy to give a little more than people expect in regard to both product and customer service.

Approaching buyers with your product is likely a brand-new experience for you, but don't let it scare you. Be confident in your idea and the quality and usefulness of your product. When you finally land a new account, large or small, offer personalized, high-quality customer service that will build long-term loyalty. Share goodwill through your company and you'll likely ensure success for years to come.

STEP
10

prep for the trade show

*Experience is a hard teacher because she gives the test first,
the lesson afterward.*

—VERNON LAW

As we discussed in the previous chapter, approaching buyers from accounts large and small is one way to begin selling. Another is to announce your product at a major industry trade show. The benefit of this approach is that you have a focused, captive audience and can create a lot of buzz in a short time. With thousands of industry-specific folks in attendance, a trade show can be the perfect place to debut your product. You will get instant feedback on your product from people who are "in the know." Your first trade show is your most important, so be prepared. It is the culmination of all of your hard work.

Choosing the Right Show

When your budget is limited, picking the right show for your debut could mean the difference between quick success and being stuck in neutral. Although there is no way to know for certain how any given show will turn out, there are many ways to make an educated guess.

With booths costing anywhere from $2,500 to $4,500 or more, when you factor in travel, lodging, shipping, food, and miscellaneous expenses, it is a really expensive decision. This makes choosing the right show all that more critical. So, how do you do that? It's simple: Do your homework. Collect all the information you can from different sources.

Some great ways to learn about shows are:

1. **From other exhibitors similar in size to your company.** If you can visit the show before your company is ready to exhibit, you will know what to expect. You will have the opportunity to meet other exhibitors and network with people who don't compete with your line. Ask them how the show has been in the past for them and how it is now. In a slow economy, buyers are attending fewer trade shows per year in order to cut back on corporate spending. So, you may want to ask buyers directly which shows they plan on attending. Although informative, another exhibitor's results may not be indicative of what *you* could do at the show, but mainly you can learn much more about the "traffic" at the show and the overall opinion or consensus of many exhibitors.

2. **Go online to the show's website and check out the exhibitor list.** Try contacting some small, noncompeting companies listed and see what you can learn about the show. You'll be surprised at how open and helpful some people will be about their trade-show experiences.

3. **Ask local store owners which shows they attend to find their new products.** Just be honest with the owner and let her know that you are trying to figure out where to exhibit your new product, and she is likely to share her insights.

4. **Ask the trade-show company to give you a list of buyers that attend the show.** They will likely give you a generic list by simply listing the stores that send buyers. Of course,

there is no guarantee that those buyers will be there or that they will stop at your booth if they are, but it is important to see the names of the companies that usually attend. If you are lucky enough to receive a list like this, try to make appointments with buyers to introduce your line. Buyers like to see new things at shows. Many times the trade-show company will pay for the big name buyers to attend the show and offer them premium travel and hotel arrangements as well. This way they can promote the fact that these buyers come to their show.

5. **Stop by your local (or call the nearest big city's) Merchandise Mart, which offer permanent showrooms.** These buildings are full of rep group showrooms (retailers come into the building to see new products from a variety of companies all under one roof) that display all different types of product lines. Sometimes these Marts have their own shows within the building. (Visit *www.merchandise martproperties.com* for more information.) Walking through the Mart can be a great experience because you can go into the showrooms and talk to the rep groups. You may need credentials to get into the building; call the local Mart to find out.

   Here are some websites for Marts in the major trade-show cities:

   - *www.lamart.com* (Los Angeles)
   - *www.americasmart.com* (Atlanta)
   - *www.merchandisemart.com* (Chicago)
   - *www.41madison.com* (New York)
   - *www.lasvegasmarket.com* (Las Vegas)

Also consider timing when choosing a show. Industry trade shows tend to be scheduled at the same time every year. The venues change for some shows, but the timing is usually the same.

million-dollar TIP Farmers' markets are trade shows, too! If you have a food-related product, they can be a great place to start. Farmers' markets generate great buzz and can even garner some valuable local press. They are an inexpensive, casual way to get consumers' reactions right on the spot and then tweak or improve your product before you exhibit "big time" at, say, a gourmet foods show. Give away lots of small samples.

Visit a Show Before You Exhibit

If you've never been to a trade show, try to attend at least one before becoming an exhibitor. In New York, Los Angeles, Chicago, or Las Vegas, this task will be easy because trade shows are held in those cities every week. If you absolutely cannot get to a show before exhibiting there, you can usually find photos of the show online or in a trade magazine, since they are usually covered by industry press.

Get In

Some shows charge a fee (the same fee they charge to attendees, which ranges from $25 to a couple hundred) for "walking" the show. You can sometimes talk your way out of the fee if you explain that you plan to exhibit your product there next year. If the initial person you speak to refuses to waive the fee, try to plead your case to upper management.

Other shows are restricted to "trade only," where you need to show credentials that prove that you are part of the industry. Have some business cards printed ahead of time so you can show them as credentials.

If you can't find a relevant trade show locally, you could even go to a "consumer" show, where businesses promote products or services directly to the consumer (rather than to buyers or owners of stores). You can find these shows advertised locally. In fact, you've probably already seen ads for shows like the "Home and Garden Show" or the "Boat Show" or the "Women's Expo." The best option is to go to one within your industry, but if you can't go to a relevant one, then try to go to any tradeshow. Almost any show will help you get familiar with the feel and pace.

Once Inside

When walking around the show, take detailed notes on the following things:

- How the booths are set up. Booths are usually set up in aisles, one right after the next, to make it easy for the buyers to visit as many as possible as quickly as possible. Some booths are open on the sides, so you can see and hear your neighbor, and some booths have walls on three sides (all except the open entrance to the aisle), which allows for much more privacy.
- How the booths are decorated. You can get lots of ideas about what you like about booth décor and what doesn't work as well.
- How the traffic flows on the trade-show floor. Note in particular the benefits of great "placement." The large companies are often positioned at key spots like right in front of the showroom door, at large intersections, and even near bathrooms.
- How people interact, and how exhibitors distribute information and samples.
- The "feel" of the show: Is it loud and exciting? Full of private conversations? Is it busy or slow? Is one product stealing the show? Some shows are more professional and "corporate," while others are more casual.

Write down your observations so you can refer back to them when it's time to set up your booth. Find out as much as you can about each show so you are prepared for the type of show you ultimately choose.

Get the Shows' Stats

When you narrow it down to a few shows you could attend, research and compare them. Call the sales agents and let them know you are considering exhibiting at the next show. Get on their mailing list and ask for a copy of the contract and a list of last year's statistics, showing who came to the show, the number of attendees, and a list of exhibitors. When you receive all the media kits and contracts, compare the shows in more detail.

How to Find Shows Within Your Industry

After you visit a sample trade show, it's time to narrow down your choices to which one you will attend. Go online and search for keywords within your industry. Broaden your search to include periphery products and stores where your product may still fit in. For example, instead of just searching for skin-care shows to exhibit Moisture Gloves, I searched "spa shows," "gift shows," and even "lingerie shows." For your first few shows, however, you should be exhibiting right in the thick of your industry.

Some trade publications publish the dates for the various industry shows. Look for a section called the "Show Directory." Search the trade papers, monthly and weekly newsletters from industry associations, and talk to people in the industry.

Who Else Is Exhibiting?

Your last step before deciding where to exhibit should be to examine the list of other exhibitors, which can usually be found under the link for "attendees" on the trade show's website. By studying the exhibitor list, you can see who else thinks it is important enough to shell out the money to exhibit at this particular show. The exhibitors you want to look for are the leaders within the industry. They bring in the important buyers. If you feel that your product needs more testing and feedback from your industry, "start small" at a local trade show that does not have the chains represented. But if you have already moved forward with marketing and manufacturing, you should be ready for the larger industry shows.

Paying to Register for the Show

Exhibiting at a trade show can cost upwards of several thousand dollars. Here are tips to help defray the initial registration cost:

- Call show management companies and inquire about discounts for first-time exhibitors (worth a try).

- If it happens to be very close to the date of the show, inquire about taking a booth that may have gotten cancelled at the last minute. Since the original exhibitor paid a nonrefundable deposit, the show would be able to charge you less and still fill the booth. (Be sure you are ready and can deliver your booth setup and products.) Since the best booth locations are taken well in advance, don't expect a good location when signing up late. In some cases, however, any location is better than missing the show.
- See if the show offers a few smaller "try me" size booths (usually sized at 5' × 10' and 8' × 10'). This is a great way to test the show at a discounted price.

In most cases, there's no way around paying the fee to exhibit. But if your product is a great fit for a particular trade show, you can't beat the exposure and buzz. You'll have to fill out a contract that outlines the fees, delivery deadlines, and other important information. I'll give you more tips for saving money on other trade-show costs later in this chapter.

Choosing Your Booth Location

Trade-show booths are considered "real estate," and the cardinal rule of location, location, location, certainly applies. If you sign up early, you sometimes have a better chance of exhibiting near the front door or near a large "anchor" booth (a large chain store or industry leader). Being close to anchors is a terrific benefit because they attract a lot of foot traffic that will have to walk by your booth.

Make Special Requests

The contract you sign with show management usually has a space for exhibitor location requests, but the task of placing hundreds or thousands of companies in a spot each one is happy with is tough. So be thoughtful about your requests and consider what's most important. The most popular request is to not be located right next to a direct competitor. The show will usually take those into consideration. However, industry trade shows usually feature several companies selling similar products. If your specific product is just one tiny offering of a bigger company's line, you may not even know that you are selling similar products until you see it at the show.

You'll see all kinds of wacky product demonstrations and personality-driven sales pitches at trade shows. Ask show management about surrounding booths when you are getting ready to sign a contract. Some shows allow exhibitors to use microphone headsets, which project sound so loudly that it's difficult to converse normally inside your booth. The same goes for loud appliances, tools, or other noisy products. Also consider nearby smells. Once we exhibited next to a company that sold incense. During the show, it made us (and other close exhibitors) truly nauseous.

Sharing a Booth

Some shows allow two companies to share a booth; others don't. When budget is an issue, you may want to consider sharing if you can find a company that has products complementary to yours. However, don't share a booth unless it is your last resort. Why?

- Booths are small (10' × 10') and you will likely feel on top of the other company.
- Shows are competitive! If you are writing orders and your booth partner isn't, he may become insecure and jealous, which makes for a really uncomfortable booth and a long three or four days.
- You or your partner may accidentally (I would hope not intentionally) take a customer away from the other mid-pitch (say your booth mate recognizes the person and says hello, for example).
- It's awkward to figure out who speaks to a passerby first.

- Booth setup is confusing. People walking by quickly may be confused because the booth is occupied by two separate companies.

You really need to know the person you would share with. People can be aggressive at shows and you want your booth to feel inviting, not crowded or intimidating. In addition, it is clear to people at the show that you're sharing for budgetary reasons, and that doesn't always send the right message. Consider all these factors long and hard before coupling up in a booth.

If You Need to Change Your Booth after You Arrive

Though it's very rare, it is not unprecedented to move your booth once you see its location during show setup. If there is an unexpected obstacle, like a pole blocking a portion of your booth, request to move before you set up. Trust me; it's easier than moving later. Speak up if you are unhappy with your booth. Because trade shows are not selling out like they used to, it's an "exhibitors market," and unsold or unused space can quickly be turned into a booth.

If they can do it, *So Can You!*

Brian Scudamore found the garbage pickup business to be very lucrative. In 1989, he started a business called the Rubbish Boys that hauled junk for people. He started out with one truck, and within a year, he was grossing $1 million. Several years later, he changed the company name to 1-800-GOT-JUNK? and began building his brand with painted trucks, clean crews dressed in uniforms, and a leadership style that made the company a real success. By 2005, revenues were $68 million, a growth of 90 percent from the previous year. Scudamore decided the best way to grow the business would be to franchise it, and today there are more than 300 1-800-GOT-JUNK? franchises in three countries.

The Difference Between Cash-and-Carry vs. Order-Only Shows

It's important to note how you'll be selling products at your show. Some shows are called cash and carry, which means that attendees can buy products at the show (for cash or credit card) and carry the goods out with them (rather than writing orders that would ship later). As an exhibitor, you can sell as much product as you can realistically bring to the show. The show is usually still a wholesale "for trade only" show, but your prospective clients can buy a sample or as many samples as they want at these type of shows without having to meet your typical order minimums.

While it is nice to physically sell products at a show, it is also costly to ship the product to the show and back home if some units don't sell. It is also difficult to calculate how much product to bring to a cash-and-carry show. There is no formula. An overestimation could be very costly. It's better to err on the side of shipping less (especially if your product is heavy). If you sell out, offer to ship the product for free for show-goers when you get home.

Other shows are "order taking only" or "writing only." No form of currency is exchanged at the show; you cannot purchase product and leave with it in hand. The order-writing-only shows are usually more professional or corporate. That is, you are more likely to get lasting accounts because the show is made up of established stores.

 Bring someone with you when you exhibit at a cash-and-carry show. You have to display a lot of product and if you run to the restroom, a less-than-honest show-goer could steal something. You need coverage in the booth at all times.

Building Your Booth From the Ground Up:
The Layout and Look

When you're officially registered for a show, it's time to design your booth. Give it some thought instead of just throwing it together with some posterboard. It's a real turnoff to walk by a booth that has a homemade sign and mismatched flooring and tables. It looks like a fly-by-night company and a buyer is not going to want to do business with someone who doesn't take pride in his or her company. You don't need a big budget to put together a nice-looking booth— you just need to take the time to sketch out ideas and pull all the elements of the booth together to make it look appealing, welcoming, and professional. Make it enticing so buyers want to visit.

The Size and Layout

The most common size booth at many trade-shows is 10' × 10'. The big companies have booths that are double or triple (or even more) that square footage. Ten by ten foot booths are a decent size to display product on two or three tables and still have a little room where people can actually "step inside" the booth to look closer or write an order.

The booth layout depends on how buyers should see and experience your product—will it be laid on a table or does it need to stand up and be moved around?

The Look of Your Booth

Setting up a booth follows the same principal as setting up a home office. First and foremost, it has to look professional. Sometimes booths are set up simply by using a round table in the middle of the booth with the new product displayed on it, along with business cards, brochure or flier, price list, and a professional-looking sign. That's it. It's an inexpensive way to make it happen—not overly impressive by any means, but simple and professional. As long as the signage and brochures are high quality, the booth can be sparse.

Build a Fake Booth

To imagine your booth, section off part of your garage, basement, or backyard with masking tape or string so you know exactly how big it is. When you've marked off the appropriate space, decide what you want to have on hand (fliers, price lists, mailing list sign-up sheet, order forms, pens, samples, chairs, tables, display cases, freebies, and so on). Then arrange everything in your fake "booth" and see if it will all fit. (Remember, rules are strict and you cannot count on another inch beyond what the show told you for a booth size.) If necessary, rearrange and reassess. This exercise also allows you to:

- Remember the little things you'll need, like a screwdriver to assemble a shelf or some specific hooks to hang a sign.
- Step back and see how your booth looks from afar (but not too far "afar"—the aisle will probably be no more than 15' wide).
- Walk by quickly and make sure that it's obvious what you're selling.
- Know how long it will take you to set up your booth.

Notes:

Be mindful about making little details count, such as keeping the color of your brochures, signage, table covering, and flooring consistent and/or complementary. Don't feel like you need an over-the-top booth with special effects and expensive furnishings before you are ready to exhibit. It is more important to spend the money on registration and be at that show with a small, but professional, presence than not be at the show. Regardless of your budget, here are some basic tips for showing your product well:

- Be sure everything is neat. You can stack things, but don't make sloppy piles.
- Place items at different levels within the booth so they're visually interesting.
- Arrange products in groups that make sense so it is easy to purchase things from the buyers' perspective. For example, if you're selling baby clothes, arrange separate pieces as outfits to entice someone to buy all parts. Visit the Container Store (*www.containerstore.com*) for storage options—they have hundreds of perfect options for helping a booth look organized.

At this point of launching your business, you cannot rely on industry buzz or your reputation to make a buyer stop, so it's critical to have clear signage and showcase your product well on your display table(s).

Signage

Above all, your booth's signage should be crystal clear about what you are selling. Buyers walk past the booths at a fast clip and they won't take the time to figure anything out, read a lot of copy, or play a guessing game. They will likely only give your booth a quick glance. The key is to make your company look real and legitimate on a shoestring budget. Luckily, this is a fairly easy task in today's high-tech world.

Signage can be made using the professional photos you had taken of your product. Find one that's large and immediately recognizable enough to use on the sign. This photo, along with your company name and logo, may be enough for a booth sign. Your graphic designer could put that together easily.

You can also use "stock" photography websites in addition to your own photos. Some good sources are:

- *www.gettyimages.com*
- *www.us.fotosearch.com*
- *www.istockphoto.com*

These sites offer beautiful, professional-quality photography covering many different scenarios (from a photo of a woman getting married, to a kid at a birthday party, to absolutely anything you can imagine). You pay a one-time fee to buy the rights to use this photo.

Of course, use the stock photos in conjunction with the photo of your product. For example, if you have a new massage tool, show it along with a stock photo of a model on a massage table. By using both, you've painted a picture of where and when your product is used. You can set the tone or theme easily with the many photos available. Some of the photos are considered "royalty free," which means you can pay for the photo once and use it on a variety of things, such as your sign and marketing materials without paying additional fees.

In addition to the look of the sign, consider the size and the material. You may be traveling to shows and need to fit the sign in your car or it will have to be packed and shipped through a carrier and there can be size limitations or higher fees for awkward packages. Also, imagine people walking by the sign may be 10 or more feet away—avoid small type at all costs.

Some sign companies print on materials that can be rolled up without wrinkling, shipped easily, and have a long lifespan. The sign is an investment in the company that you will be able to use for many shows to come, and maybe even years to come, so make something you are proud to display. You will be standing in front of it and it will represent your product and company.

Pull It All Together

Once you have determined the main parts of your booth (furniture, signage, product display), think about adding some small touches to bring the design up a notch. For example, try a nice tableskirt that matches your color scheme, an extra lighting fixture, or piece of furniture that can double as storage space.

As long as the booth is professional looking and clearly showcases your products, you don't need a special theme or excessive staging, so don't go overboard.

Packing and Shipping Your Booth to the Show

Since you've completed the Biz Brainstorm: Build a Fake Booth exercise (on page 205), you know exactly what you need to bring to the show. Compile everything and begin packing it in a way that will be logical when you unpack and set up your booth. For example, if you need a screwdriver to assemble a shelf, either pack it with the shelf or with a small tool bag. Plan ahead so you avoid throwing items into random boxes. Here are some items you probably need. You will, of course, have some other supplies so be sure to add them to the list.

Trade-show Supplies Checklist
○ Box cutter
○ Business cards
○ Carpet/flooring (unless the show will provide that for you)
○ Display product, samples, and testers
○ Fabric for tables and/or backdrop
○ Fliers, brochures, price sheets, and press kits
○ Hand cart/dolly
○ Press coverage in magazines for display
○ Purchase order forms (in duplicate; buyers will want a copy)
○ Return shipping labels
○ Ribbons, frames, and decorative accessories
○ Scissors, pens, note pads

○ Sheets or tarps (to cover booth at night)
○ Signage
○ Snacks, water, gum, and mints
○ Staple gun (if necessary for stapling heavy-duty fabric to tables, for example), extra staples
○ Stapler, extra staples
○ Tables or other furniture needed
○ Tape (regular, masking, double-sided, and shipping)
○ And, last but not least: a copy of your trade-show contract (Occasionally the show may assign you a different booth number than was on your contract. So, keep it handy along with any other addendums or changes you may have made.)

The more prepared you are, the smoother your setup will go and the more energy you'll have for the show itself. Once you have your components packed, do the following things before shipping:

• Make a list of each carton's tracking number and its contents. Since you'll probably be shipping on multiple days it's easy to forget what you've already shipped. Also, if you are missing a box or package when you get there, you'll know all the things that were in the missing box. You'll know which box you packed your scissors or box cutters in so you can open that box first. Trying to open well-taped boxes with your belt buckle or a pen is embarrassing and difficult.

• Write your exhibitor name and booth number with a bold black marker or preprinted stickers *all over* each box and package. This makes it easier for the warehouse workers to get it to your booth because they won't have to focus on one small label. It will also help locate a package in the facility if it gets lost.

• Prepare labels to return the boxes. Preprint the return labels, on label sheets, preferably, so you just have to peel and stick. You will love the time this saves getting out. Keep these labels and your trade-show contract together in a folder. Be just as organized to leave as you are to arrive.

Also, consider how you're getting to the show. If you're driving, you may want to take a few essentials in the car with you so that in the unfortunate event that a box or two is lost, you are not without, say, your product!

million-dollar **TIP**

Cover your booth each night. Although the show will provide security during off-hours, you do hear of rare occasions where products are stolen from booths. Almost every booth will "lock up" by covering merchandise with sheets. Go to Target or any discount store and get a few king-sized flat sheets (the fitted sheets are no help at all) on the clearance rack to drape over your booth.

Bringing the Booth to the Show Yourself

If you didn't have to ship your booth supplies to the show site, consider yourself lucky. You will have everything in your own hands and you will save a lot of money. Obviously, the cheapest way to get your booth to a show is to haul it to the show, unload it, and get it to your booth location yourself. Exhibition facilities make the "schlepper" option fairly easy, as long as you obey their instructions and don't ask them for manual labor or supplies.

Larger shows will usually have a "set up" day prior to the show day when exhibitors can pull up, park, and unload their booth materials without too much trouble. For example, the day before a show at the Jacob Javits Center in New York City, you can park your vehicle right in front of the building free of charge and unload your booth. The biggest hassle is waiting for an elevator. Not too bad.

Some facilities make it even easier for the "schlepper." At a recent show at the Los Angeles Convention Center, exhibitors simply pulled up to the rear of the facility on set-up day, unloaded everything onto waiting pallets and forklift drivers delivered the pallets to their booth locations without a charge. What a rare pleasure!

But don't count on that type of treatment. In fact, don't expect the facility (or fellow schleppers) to provide anything except an open door. It's not like pulling up to a hotel with luggage carts lying around and someone to haul your stuff for a tip. You're truly on your own if you choose this option. Dress accordingly. Plan on it being the opposite of what you want it to be because the facility isn't turning on the air conditioning or heating yet because all the doors are open to the outside all day.

Invest in a Hand Truck

Convention centers are vast, enormous facilities. The distance from your vehicle to the booth location can be hundreds of yards or easily even more. This makes the schlepper's most important tool (often overlooked by the first-time exhibitor) a quality, collapsible cart, also called a "hand truck." You can get a lightweight, collapsible, aluminum hand truck with elastic straps for about $100. Make sure it's collapsible so it can fit under a booth table or in an overhead compartment on a plane. Don't skimp. The only sight more pathetic than watching a first-time exhibitor searching in vain to borrow a hand truck is watching someone struggle with a flimsy luggage cart with toy-car-sized wheels. Been there, done that. I once had to retrace my steps back down aisles to find the screws from the wheels on my hand truck. Don't make my mistake.

The key to having a successful trade-show experience is to choose the best show for your product, then be organized and prepared. Trade shows are expensive, so treat it with a level of importance that equals your financial investment and the potential for the show to put your product on the map. Spend your time organizing beforehand, so that at the show, you can focus on just selling and networking.

make your trade show debut

Expect the best. Prepare for the worst. Capitalize on what comes.

—ZIG ZIGLAR

As you enter the exhibit hall on the first day of your first trade show, it is a memorable moment. You have entered the arena; you are a player. Picture it for minute: Visualize yourself walking into the huge room with all those booths and all those businesses, and see your booth among them. You have done it. What a feeling! You have a product for the marketplace and now is your chance to tell everyone about it. Here are tips for making the most of your debut.

Trade Show Dos and Don'ts

Yes, it's from *Annie*, but it's true: You're never fully dressed without a smile. Come to the show confident, prepared, energetic, and enthusiastic. The new booths get a lot of attention at shows, so let your positive energy be contagious!

Dress the Part

Remember one word about appropriate dress for a trade show: comfort. As business owners, we probably sit at a desk or computer for a good part of the day. At trade shows, you will stand for at least eight to ten hours a day for several days. It is a big change.

The first priority is sensible shoes. Be fashionable, but trust me, choose comfort over style. At every show, inevitably, I see a woman wearing pointy-toed stiletto heels. She's usually limping around by hour five of the first day. If at all possible, don't buy new shoes for the occasion. Bring some shoes you know are comfortable that look professional and clean.

Once you have your comfortable shoes (and extra Band-Aids just in case), focus on your outfit. The attire depends on the show. For example, for the corporate shows, choose a more conservative business attire. For the more informal shows, go with business-casual. You could embroider your company logo onto nice shirts, which will eliminate any clothing dilemmas and anyone working in the booth will have the same "uniform" look.

Avoid attire that is racy or has the potential to offend someone. People can be judgmental and why risk turning off a buyer? Even if she likes your product, she may feel intimidated to step into your tiny ten-by-ten booth and talk with you if you are overexposed or wearing a shirt with a certain political slogan. Use common sense and your best judgment. When in doubt, err on the more dressed-up and conservative side. After all, you are there first and foremost to do business, so dress as you would for a business interview.

Stay Positive

Maintaining a positive attitude and high energy level for the length of the show is not always easy, but you have to do it. You'll need plenty of inner strength. By the last part of the first day, you still have to look fresh whether you have had much traffic in your booth or not, or even written an order. Take a deep breath and keep your hopes up. Be prepared with your own mantras (positive sayings) that you can repeat to yourself to bring your mind back to that positive, happy place.

If you're not alone manning the booth, leave for a bit and walk around, take deep breaths, stretch a little, and return refreshed. If you are alone, you can usually walk up and down your aisle to take a breather and still keep an eye on the booth. (Yes, the booth is like an infant who cannot be left alone!)

If a show's traffic is slow, other exhibitors start to complain, and we all know that misery loves company. Negativity can spread like the flu. Stay positive and maintain high energy, even in those situations. Anything can change in a flash, and the buyer from that large chain store may be just around the corner. You don't want him to hear you whining to your neighbor. A few years ago, as I was literally packing up my boxes at the close of a dud of a show, a man in a suit walked into the booth, and started asking me questions about my products. By this time, I was a tad depressed, tired, and not in the mood to chit-chat. It turned out this last-minute visitor owned one of the largest mail-order catalogs in the nail care industry. He placed an order and became a client for several years.

If they can do it, *So Can You!*

The following are billion (with a B!)-dollar privately held (for profit!) American companies that are still run by someone from the founding family. Do you think these entrepreneurs thought they had a product or service idea that would last generations?

- Enterprise Rent-A-Car
- Gallo Winery
- Hallmark Cards
- Hearst Newspapers
- Koehler Plumbing
- Levi Strauss
- Marriott
- Mary Kay Cosmetics
- Perdue Farms
- Viacom

How to Eat During the Show

I know this heading sounds funny, but food can really affect your energy level and energy is vital during a long show. Trade shows are endurance tests—think marathon, not sprint. Eating at shows can be tricky (remember, you can't easily leave your booth unmanned), so it is best to be prepared. Consider bringing your food—you get to eat what you like and you don't waste time in line at the convention center restaurant buying overpriced food that makes you feel sluggish.

If You're Alone

If you are alone in your booth, pack food for the day and keep it in a small cooler. It can be really uncomfortable to try to take bites of food in between booth visitors and it would be embarrassing to get caught with a mouthful of food and not be able to answer a question. Also, food can quickly "stink" up the booth. But if you're alone, there's not much you can do but buy or bring food that's easy and neat to eat (no sloppy sandwiches) and doesn't have a strong smell. My favorites are fruit salad, yogurt, and trail mixes.

If You Have Help

If you have a friend or spouse working with you in the booth, eat your quick meals at a table in the show lobby. You'll get a precious few minutes of time away from the booth.

Don't Drink Too Much

Unfortunately, the food and discipline regimen does not end when the show closes in the evening. Don't go overboard on the alcohol to celebrate or commiserate. As you can imagine, standing in the booth the next day for eight to ten hours feeling tired and a bit hungover is a nightmare.

Keep Your Dinners Boring

Don't try any new foods at dinner after the show—you do not want any stomach issues the following day. Try to eat a light, healthy dinner with foods that you know agree with you. Also, try to not eat foods that "stay" with you, like garlic.

It took me years to realize that the shows are not a vacation. They are more like a three-day job interview. So if these suggestions sound really boring, especially if you are in a fun city like Vegas or Manhattan, all I can say is I've lived it and learned.

Make Trade Show Friends

On set-up day, the atmosphere is casual and laid-back. Everyone is dressed in jeans or sweats and sneakers, and it's fun to chat with people while setting up your booth. It's a good idea to set up first thing in the morning so you can be done by midday to wander around the floor and check out other booths.

If you continue to exhibit your product at shows, you'll likely see the same faces again and again, so it's worth it to invest a few minutes to meet some people. I have made a group of friends at trade shows who mean a lot to me. We swap trade-show stories and laugh about mistakes, problems, or even buyers that we encounter during shows. It's like being part of a support group.

Also, consider the show an opportunity to network with others who don't compete with you. They are usually surprisingly honest and open. Then you get the opportunity to help other entrepreneurs. The friendship fuels a feeling of camaraderie instead of fierce competition.

Give Show Samples and Discounts

You likely have samples of your product on hand for occasions just like this. If you can't give them away, you still have many tactics you can use to help garner a sale.

SAMPLES

Everyone loves samples at shows. If your product is not something you can give away, find a way to let people test it out at the show or give small samples. Without a sample, a buyer won't know how good your product is and they may instead buy from the company whose sample they tried.

When I show Moisture Gloves at shows, I can't give away a pair to everyone, but we have lots of samples on display for people to try on. Of course, we do give a sample to an interested buyer of a large company or an editor of a magazine. If you can't give away samples, offer incentive pricing and throw in a free product for the buyer with an order that can serve as their sample.

SHOW SPECIALS

At a trade show, consider offering buyers a special deal to entice them to order. Offer a deal you thought of ahead of time to help to make sales and open new accounts. Try a "show special" that showcases a variety of your products and makes it simple to open a new account without having the buyer make too many decisions.

This is the beauty of having your own business. You tailor the show special to what best suits your inventory and manufacturing situation at the moment. A trade-show special can be anything from free shipping on an order over a certain dollar amount, a percentage discount on product, a giveaway display case, or anything you can think of as incentive. Figure out what costs you the least amount of money, but still seems like a true savings or benefit to the buyer. For example, if you offer free shipping, know that you will have to pay more on the UPS account that month. It's often better to offer a discount and move out inventory at a lower profit margin than have it sitting in your "warehouse."

You may also encounter buyers who try to negotiate their own show special with things that are important to them, such as longer terms on an invoice (say, Net 60 rather than Net 30) in addition to pricing discounts. You'll need to think on your feet (in your comfy, rubber-soled, trade-show shoes, that is) and figure out if it is better to break even on the sale and land this new account, or not make a sale at all.

Develop Your Daily Trade-Show Routine

Each morning, before you leave your hotel room, be sure you are stocked up with purchase orders, pens, business cards, brochures, and anything that may have been used up the day before. Be prepared with lots of handouts for each day of the show.

Get to the booth at least thirty minutes before the show opens to freshen up the booth. Sometimes a sign can fall down or a display may have been knocked over, so leave a little time for the unexpected. Use the extra time to walk around and see the show—you likely haven't had time to walk the entire floor yet. If you see a booth that carries a similar or competing product to yours, figure out the differences and your benefits. Introduce yourself to other exhibitors; get to know people.

Exhibitors usually arrive twenty to thirty minutes before the show starts. While they are drinking coffee, they may be open to conversation. Like set-up day, the mood is casual in the mornings. When the show is over at the end of the day everyone races out, so that early morning is the best time to meet people.

GIVE OUT PROMOTIONAL ITEMS

A lot of exhibitors give out inexpensive promotional gifts to keep their company name in front of a buyer. High quality pens, sticky notes, and tote bags are practical options, which can be emblazoned with your company name and/or logo.

Investigate your options at least four weeks prior to the show to have the products ready in time. Visit these websites for ideas: *www.thepromotouch.com*, *www.bestimpressions.com*, and *www.epromos.com*.

Collect Business Cards

Place a basket on one of your tables and invite people to drop in their business cards. Ask for a business card from anyone that stops at the booth, even other exhibitors. Ask if it's okay to add them to your mailing list (or have a sign indicating that's the purpose). Voilà, you have begun your customer database. Keep a spare notebook to keep track of information in case someone doesn't have a card. You can also use this basket to have a drawing on the last day of the show for a giveaway . . . people can usually find a business card if it's for a giveaway.

million-dollar **TIP** Jot down quick notes on business cards so when you call to follow up, you can mention the specifics of how they said they would introduce the product. Some people say "I would love to have these for a Mother's Day promo" or "These would be perfect for our seminar on reflexology." You will be grateful for those notes. Once you are away from the trade show you won't remember the comments but you can remind them of what they said at the show—you're likely to get the order!

Protect Yourself from Trade Show Predators

My husband refers to trade shows as the "den of thieves" and though it sounds harsh, it's with good reason. His work on cases of trademark infringement has tainted him. Whenever anyone has a great product idea and is about to tell someone about it, they always preface it with these words: "Don't tell anyone, promise?" The fear of someone stealing the idea is real. This reason alone is why many people just hold onto their ideas. They figure that they will make the effort and then a big huge Goliath company will come along and mass-produce it as they are slowly making progress.

It happens often. Someone brings a new innovation to the marketplace and it gets copied. In fact, expect it if you are successful.

The only answer is to be protected with your intellectual property rights. In conversations, only divulge information about the product itself. Never discuss trade secrets or proprietary information such as the manufacturing process, design, cost, and profit margin. No one at the show needs to know any of those things.

Enjoy the Experience

With all the hard work it took to get there, you may forget to enjoy the experience. Every show is worthwhile in ways that may not always be obvious during the show. If the show didn't open as many new accounts as you had hoped for, you probably then had a chance to network more and meet a new trade-show friend. Sometimes months down the road, someone you spoke with at the show contacts you and gives you an order or a referral. The purchase orders do not always materialize at that moment.

million-dollar **TIP** You shake a lot of hands at trade shows, so never be caught with a weak handshake. It immediately conveys weakness and also distracts attention from what you may want to say, as the recipient of a weak shake may be thinking about why that just occurred. Speaking of shaking hands, you may want to keep hand sanitizer in your booth. You don't want to catch a cold from someone, so it pays to use these cleansers throughout the duration of the show.

The effort that you make to meet buyers and network with exhibitors is always valuable. So, while you are there, "work" the show. Take advantage of the fact that you are in a room with other people that are active in the same industry. Learn. Experience. Take it in.

Leaving the Show

When it's time to wrap up, pack your booth into boxes. Be glad you have come organized and prepared with preprinted address stickers to save time. You may see bargain hunters, who walk around at the very end of the show to see if exhibitors want to sell samples cheaply, so they do not have to pay to ship it back. You can sell as much or as little as you want.

The Show Aftermath: Follow-Up

The show has ended—now the real work begins! If you didn't garner a lot of orders at the show, here are some tips to turn the leads into future sales:

- Make a database from the business cards you received or scanned.
- E-mail those contacts and thank them for visiting your booth.
- After a few weeks, e-mail them again and offer to re-extend the show special or offer a discount on their initial order. They will have paid off the trade-show bills and it may be a better time for them to purchase some products that they were interested in.
- Ask them for feedback on your product. Maybe they didn't place an order because of one simple thing that you can remedy for them.
- Make up a new postcard and mail it to the database a couple of months later. They will see the product in a new light.

If someone was interested enough to come into your booth and give you a business card, he or she should be considered a good lead. Be in touch with as many of the attendees as possible at some point. You may learn how you can improve for the next show.

Look for companies that rent scanners to exhibitors at trade shows so that you can scan their badges instead of collecting a card. The scanner companies work in conjunction with show management, so you receive all the critical contact information from the person. If it's a busy show with a lot of attendees, it's a good idea to use a scanner system if the rental rate is reasonable (it can go as high as $300). It'll be a big timesaver and you know the information is correct. The downside is that you can't write notes on the back of a card you don't have. So you have to take better notes.

Should You Hire a Sales Representative?

When the show results were not as good as expected, some people may ask themselves this question. Working with a rep may help spread the news about your brand faster than you can alone. However, if you just have one or two products, your line may get lost in the rep's assortment of other, larger lines. Reps like lines that have lots of SKUs because they make the most money with those brands.

How the Financial Arrangement Works

Since many reps make no money unless they actually sell your products, you really have nothing to lose. Start with a three- to six-month contract. Sales reps charge approximately 15 percent commission on orders that they write for your company. If they open an account and receive a purchase order for $1,000, the rep is paid $150. Some reps get paid once you have received your payment from the company; others request payment on the 1st or 15th of every month, whether you have been paid or not. If, for some reason, an account cancels and you have already paid the rep, deduct it from the next check.

Rep groups will show their lines at trade shows, so you can often visit some you are considering. A rep group will charge you a fee (several hundred dollars) on top of their commission to have your products in their booth at a show. Sometimes this may be the only affordable option to have a small presence at a show.

How to Find a Good Rep

If you want to use a sales rep group, use your researching skills, which are no doubt finely honed now. Try these tactics:

- Get a referral from another company that has been successful with the rep firm.
- Put a sign up in your booth at the trade show. Reps within the industry usually walk the shows and will see you're interested.
- If you see a product that is complementary to yours (not competitive) and is sold in the stores that you want your product to be in, contact that company and ask who reps their line.
- Check websites for products that are complementary to yours. Some companies have their rep information on their website.
- Go to the closest big city and walk the showrooms or Mart buildings (see Step 10 for more on Marts). There, you can see all the lines that a rep has and see if your line fits into his or her assortment. (You can also usually go to the Mart's website and search for products and see who reps them.) Set up some appointments before going to the Mart.

Trade shows are a really terrific way to launch your product and give it the exposure it deserves within the industry. Exhibiting at a trade show makes you feel like a part of your industry. You've arrived. If you are organized and prepared, you will be ready to put your best foot forward and begin a major marketing campaign at the show. Who knows, you could leave with a really, really big purchase order! Just knowing that it's possible makes it exciting.

STEP

12

maintain a life balance and look ahead

In the midst of movement and chaos, keep stillness within you.

—DEEPAK CHOPRA

Now that you're well on your way to bringing your idea to life, keep in mind that life is all about balance. While launching your product requires many sacrifices, it's the most organized and responsible among us who can work and still maintain relationships and a measure of good health. Balancing all of your commitments gracefully and responsibly while starting a new business takes a lot of effort. Life is a juggling act at "regular" times, let alone when you're trying to start a business. Time management and stress relief are two important ways to keep balanced.

With a lot on your plate, you may find yourself burning the candle at both ends, which eventually leads to burnout and sleep deprivation. Having it all without becoming overwhelmed and over-committed is the name of the game. It is a trial-and-error process as you welcome this new venture into your life. Some days will be completely smooth, perfect, and very productive, and other days . . . well, they won't be so great. If you're calm and organized, you'll be better equipped to monitor the big picture of your product line and consider ways it can grow in upcoming years. The following strategies may help you.

Observing "Office Hours" Inside Your Home Office

Efficient time management starts with a basic idea—keeping office hours as *office* hours. Seems easy, right? Well, it can be difficult when you hear the goings-on in other parts of the house or your home phone is ringing.

Try this simple, yet effective, tip: Don't pick up your home or cell phone during your business hours even though you are at home. With caller ID you can check to see if it's an emergency call from your kids' school; if not, voice mail will cover for you. Friends may feel that they can call you at home to discuss anything (or nothing), but they wouldn't bother you at your office with just a "hello" call. If you answer those calls, you're allowing someone else to cut into your work progress. You don't need to be unsociable—just utilize those work hours for work only. Socialize during designated free time.

You will see how productive you can be when you can work without interruption. When you don't allow miscellaneous distractions, you will become uber-efficient, completing lots of tasks in a small chunk of time.

Scheduling Will Help You Work Smart

You don't necessarily need to work *harder* to get more done, you need to work smarter. Planning will help you accomplish that goal. Map out your schedule for the day, week, and even the month. Write a list of tasks and goals to accomplish and stick to the priorities. Think about short- and long-term goals. Sometimes you can get into such a crazy pace trying to juggle everything that you lose focus on the big picture and are just caught up with the minutiae. Try to look at the big picture of your business and your life at the end of every day or at least at the end of every week. Take a few minutes to reassess and make a new list of tasks.

Buy a giant calendar from an office supply store and fill it in weekly. Or, use your computer's calendar program to set reminders of what needs to be done. If you assign a task to a specific day, you are more likely to do it then.

Set Some Goals to Achieve

Here are some questions to help you think about goals you want to achieve. Fill in the answers:

Within one month, my goals are:_____

Due date: _____

I will reward myself when I achieve these goals by: _____

_____

Within three months, my goals are: _____

Due date: _____

I will reward myself when I achieve these goals by: _____

_____

Within six months, my goals are: _____

Due date: _____

_____

I will reward myself when I achieve these goals by: _____

_____

Within one year, my goals are: _____

Due date: _____

I will reward myself when I achieve these goals by: _____

_____

Celebrate your successes! And then begin a new list.

The system you use isn't what's important; it's that you are focused and prioritize. If you wander into your office every day without a plan, you'll end up working reactively. While you certainly need to deal with whatever fires come up that day, you also need to make progress on planned tasks. That balance isn't easy to achieve, but if you're actively aware of it, you're more likely to accomplish it.

Act "As If" to Motivate Yourself

Motivational speakers often speak of acting "as if" you are already the person you are dreaming to be. This psychological game may sound silly, but it can have a profound effect on your mindset. For example, I acted "as if" my business already had clients and it made me feel responsible to a real entity, not just this abstract idea of my product.

Sanity-Saving Tips

You probably think you're already making the most of every moment in your day. Well, in order to manage this new venture and your personal life, you need to streamline even further. You *can* find time for (almost) everything if you manage your schedule well and keep a healthy mind and energetic body. Set your priorities and boundaries and stick to them. Listen to your body; if you are dragging and exhausted, take a rest. Don't feel guilty about taking the time you need to get back into balance. The following ideas may help.

Find Ways to Save Time

Look for ways to save time in your everyday life. For example, use a hands-free headset and talk to friends while doing laundry, cleaning the house, or cooking dinner. Use your cell phone (with a hands-free headset) to talk while running errands or driving in the car (if you can drive and talk without getting distracted).

Act As If You Are . . .

Write down a detailed description of the person you hope to be when your product is out there in the marketplace. Think about the feel of the day, the event that you will be dreaming about (receiving a purchase order from Target, or cashing a six-figure check, or showing your spouse the purchase order), and write down anything you can think of that will motivate you to work toward actually feeling this day in reality. Then visualize it in your mind and act as if that event has happened. Be proud of your business. Go back to this visualization daily to refuel your desire.

E-mail and/or text message people when possible to save time on phone calls with people who like to chat when you may not necessarily have time. I have arranged carpools, play dates, and lunch dates by e-mail or texting in a fraction of the time it would have taken by phone. I don't mean to sound antisocial, but your time is limited as you launch a new business, so look at it as being more efficient, not less social. Your friends should understand.

If they can do it, So Can you!

Actor/comedian Jim Carrey tells a story of acting "as if" he was successful when he was a struggling comic without much money. In 1987, he wrote himself a $10 million check from his own checking account (which was nearly empty). He postdated it for 1995, and eagerly anticipated the day he could cash it. Sure enough, by the time 1995 came around, he was earning $20 million per film. Try his tactic: Postdate a check to yourself with an amount that would thrill you in five years. Keep the check in plain sight as you work hard.

Learn to Say "No"

Volunteer for things that are meaningful to you, but don't feel you have to say "yes" to everyone who comes to you asking for favors. Your time is valuable and you need to be protective of it. If you are too busy, let the requester know that you have too many obligations at the moment, but would be happy to volunteer your time later (if possible, give a specific time—next month, in July, after Thanksgiving, etc.). It's liberating to say "no for now." People understand and appreciate your honesty. Besides, it's better to wait than take on a cause and not give it the attention it deserves.

Make Time for Exercise

You've heard it a million times from your doctor, on TV, and in magazines. Exercise is good for you. Try to exercise at least three to four times a week. I know—when will you have time for that? Think of exercise like eating and sleeping; you need it in your schedule, it's non-negotiable. Choose whatever exercise works for you. If you don't have access to gym equipment, simply grab your iPod and take a brisk twenty-minute walk. You'll feel stronger after exercise—both emotionally and physically.

million-dollar **TIP** As you streamline your schedule and sacrifice social time for work, make the effort to find *some* time to spend with friends. Whether you meet for a walk or a coffee date, getting away from it all can be rejuvenating. In fact, studies show that being with our favorite friends has a positive effect on our nervous system. So take time for laughter and friendship.

Don't Worry

Try to let go of the unnecessary worries of the day. They say that a day of worry is more exhausting than a week of work (I agree!). If you get consumed with worry, refocus on your goals. I give you this advice as a former worrier, so I know what it's like. The message of some motivational speakers helped me—I like Tony Robbins and Deepak Chopra. If motivational speakers don't work for you, listen to music or meditate. Find a way to let go of thoughts that aren't serving you well. Again, the system isn't what's important—what matters is that you let it go.

To start letting go of worry, simply catch yourself when you begin worrying. Try to shift gears. Instead of thinking about what you didn't do or what you don't have, focus on what you have accomplished and the fact that you are following a dream. Cleanse your mind daily by taking some deep breaths. With each exhale let some "stuff" go.

Involve Your Friends and Family

I mentioned involving friends and family back in Step 1, but at this point, they can help you with the business instead of nonbusiness tasks. Ask friends and family to help you assembling press kits, packaging product, or affixing SKU stickers. Maybe you haven't been able to socialize or maybe they haven't fully understood what you have been working on. If so, this is a great opportunity for your biggest supporters to feel involved. Be sure you reward them as much as possible—pay for pizza and drinks. If you make it fun and reward them nicely, they may even return to "work" with you again.

Tips Your Mother Probably Told You

Yes, she was right!

- **Get out of your comfort zone every now and then.** Drive a different route to your kids' school or a meeting. Try not to be a creature of habit *all* the time; get some new perspective.
- **Don't get sloppy doing simple tasks.** If you do things too fast, you may not do them correctly. You don't want to have to do things twice, so don't move at a crazy, frenetic pace just to check things off the list. Do things right and mindfully the first time.
- **Keep positive.** Surround yourself with supportive people. When you run into a problem, know you will find a solution. It's not about what you *can't* do. It's about what you *will* do to make things happen.
- **Say goodbye to guilt.** There are just twenty-four hours in the day. Do the best you can. If you didn't accomplish everything you had hoped for, move remaining tasks to your list for the next day.

million-dollar **TIP** Don't underestimate the value of silence. Get in the car and don't turn on the radio. Eat without watching TV. The silence can be very relaxing. The rejuvenating benefits of a few minutes of silence during the day can last hours.

Product Line Expansion

If you're able to achieve a healthy work/life balance, you'll find that you have time to plan for the future of your product or business. Isn't that exciting? Not only do you have a product; it has a future!

Consider how to expand your product into a line of products or a variety of one specific product. For example, if you are launching a new baby bottle, think about producing other baby-feeding products. You could also think about different designs, patterns, and nuances for the one bottle.

As you expand your line and/or your business, you still need to continue to run a tight ship as far as employees, inventory, and cash flow in order to keep profit margin levels the same. What's the point of getting more business if you are not making more money? You will end up working twice as hard for half the money if you don't constantly re-evaluate the systems and production costs that you have in place. You *can* expand your product line and/or customer accounts without adding personnel or having to lease real office space. You may need to have a bigger storage unit or upgrade your software programs but bigger gross sales numbers do not always translate to bigger margins if there are too many other costs associated with the growth.

At Moisture Jamzz, I began with one design of our Moisture Gloves and then added more fabric designs so people would want to own more than one pair of the same product. A few years into the business, people asked, "What else do you do besides the gloves?" The answer was "nothing." That got me thinking about expansion ideas, and we now offer socks, gift baskets, and other items that complement our original product.

The same thing will probably happen to you. Once your product is doing well, your customers will ask if you have anything else and larger retailers will want to display more than one lonely product. Take advantage of your brand's success and loyalty and continue

Ideas for Expansion

Jot down ideas about possible product expansions. Think about both new items that would complement your current product and also variations of the original product, perhaps something that is customized or personalized. What changes can you make to appeal to more people?

----

to grow. By then, the process of adding to your line will seem easy because you know how to do it and you know that you *can* do it. You have built relationships with your graphic designer, your manufacturing and packaging sources, and the buyers. Everything is in place for future growth.

There are many ways to get product expansion ideas, such as:

1. **Creative thinking:** Ideas may just come to you as you use and sell your own product in situations that are different than you originally imagined. Keep an open mind.

2. **Trade-show feedback:** People who visit your booth at trade shows may make valuable suggestions. People love to express ideas of how to improve your product and what should come next. The suggestions are frequently good, as these people like the product and want to see even more from you.

3. **Buyers:** As you present your idea to retail buyers, they will usually give you constructive feedback. They might suggest that you offer more varieties of your product, or more complementary items to offer a more complete line.

4. **Your customers:** Post a link to your e-mail address on your website so customers or visitors can leave suggestions or comments. These can be very insightful.

5. **Spot trends:** Be keenly aware of trends in the news, both in your industry and in the marketplace as a whole. Staying tuned into current events could lead to a new product idea or product extension and can help you locate an untapped market niche. For example, food allergies have become very common. Companies saw a recent surge in peanut allergies in children, and targeted this demographic by making soy butter and almond butter. Be timely. What about a green or organic version of your product? Can you incorporate solutions to these new current issues by making some changes to your product? With your finger on the pulse

of hot products, you can even piggyback, like Jibbitz did to Crocs. Piggybacking means creating a complementary product for an already-successful product.

As you launch your product, you are your own teacher in many ways. No matter how many books you read or how much advice you are given, nothing can replace rolling up your sleeves and learning firsthand, step by step. Some parts of your journey will be easy and fun, and you will feel a sense of accomplishment immediately. Other phases will be longer, frustrating, disappointing, and difficult. Realize that this roller coaster is normal and move through the challenging times. Your personal "end of the rainbow" vision will keep you going. Let go of excuses; you picked up this book for a reason, it's now time for *Your Idea, Inc.*!

There is nothing like the feeling of seeing your product on the shelves in the stores. There is nothing like the feeling of hearing from a customer who loves and needs your product. There is nothing like the feeling of being your own boss. Remember: If I can do it, so can you!

conclusion

My dreams as I wrote this book were twofold. First, I wanted to see it in its finished form—clean, crisp, edited, and in the bookstores. I carried my vision of this book in my head for years until I made the choice to take action. Second, I dreamed of being at a book signing and seeing a sea of my books completely opposite to what I just described. No longer new, crisp, and clean but instead worn in, written all over, with dog-eared pages full of Post-it Notes. I dream of seeing this book literally transform itself from my journey to yours.

Please help me to realize my dream by fulfilling yours. Now go take action!

index

about the author

SANDY ABRAMS is founder and CEO of Moisture Jamzz, Inc. Founded in 1993 around her signature moisturizing glove product, Moisture Jamzz has counted among its clients Bath & Body Works; the Estée Lauder Company (Origins and Aveda); H2O PLUS; Crabtree & Evelyn; Bare Escentuals; Bed, Bath, & Beyond; Linens 'n Things; Stroud's; Williams-Sonoma's Chambers Catalog; Bloomingdale's; and QVC. Moisture Jamzz products can be found in some of the finest spas, resorts, skin-care salons, and beauty supply stores throughout the world. Sandy's products have been featured by editors in many of the top lifestyle publications such as *In Style*, *The New York Times*, *Glamour*, *Shape*, *Cosmo*, *Redbook*, *Modern Bride*, and *Beauty Launchpad*.

Without a business degree, Sandy started in a corner of her one-bedroom Los Angeles apartment and built Moisture Jamzz, Inc. from scratch into a company grossing millions of dollars. Today, it is still a privately held corporation that Sandy runs with her husband.